Perspectives on Intercultural Psychotherapy

In *Perspectives on Intercultural Psychotherapy*, Okeke Azu-Okeke explores cultural identity by drawing on his own experience as the first and only Black trainee in an Institute for Group Analysis in London and the impact this has had on his work as a lecturer and supervisor, as well as research from his group analysis sessions over many years to contribute a deeper awareness of the serious aspects of colonialism.

Drawing from the perspective of an Igbo man of the older generation who grew up in two conflicting cultures, the traditional Igbo culture of Nigeria and that of the British colonialists, Okeke provides a thorough study of how cultural identity can influence research and practice in whatever form it takes: the academic, the theoretical, the economic and the psychological. The book discusses how ignoring deeply held social and spiritual values can alienate many trainees and potential clients from participating in the professions of psychotherapy and counselling. It also reflects on the author's research into traditional Igbo methods of healing and compares these with Western models, especially of group analysis, and discusses how mutual learning can be achieved.

This book will be of great interest to counsellors and psychotherapists; arts therapists; sociologists and anthropologists; policy makers engaged in health and social care policies; practitioners of alternative medicine; social workers and mental health workers at all levels.

Okeke Azu-Okeke has an MA in Deviancy and Social Policy from Middlesex University, UK. He has wide experience as a mental health professional in radical NHS centres such as the Henderson Hospital Surrey, the Aro Centre Nigeria, and as a group analytic psychotherapist, teacher, supervisor and innovator.

Explorations in Mental Health

Depressive Realism
Interdisciplinary perspectives
Colin Feltham

Families Bereaved by Alcohol or Drugs
Coping and Support
Edited by Christine Valentine

Trans and Sexuality
An Existentially-informed Enquiry with Implications for Counselling Psychology
Christina Richards

Narratives of Loneliness
Multidisciplinary Perspectives from the 21st Century
Edited by Olivia Sagan and Eric D. Miller

Evil Eye, Jinn Possession, and Mental Health Issues
An Islamic Perspective
G. Hussein Rassool

Africana Peoples in China
Psychoanalytic Perspectives on Migration Experiences, Identity, and Precarious Employment
C. Jama Adams

Perspectives on Intercultural Psychotherapy
An Igbo Group Analyst's Search for Social and Cultural Identity
Okeke Azu-Okeke

For more information about this series, please visit www.routledge.com/Explorations-in-Mental-Health/book-series/EXMH

Perspectives on Intercultural Psychotherapy

An Igbo Group Analyst's Search for Social and Cultural Identity

Okeke Azu-Okeke

LONDON AND NEW YORK

First published 2019
by Routledge
2 Park Square, Milton Park, Abingdon, Oxon OX14 4RN

and by Routledge
52 Vanderbilt Avenue, New York, NY 10017

Routledge is an imprint of the Taylor & Francis Group, an informa business

© 2019 Okeke Azu-Okeke

The right of Okeke Azu-Okeke to be identified as author of this work has been asserted by him in accordance with sections 77 and 78 of the Copyright, Designs and Patents Act 1988.

All rights reserved. No part of this book may be reprinted or reproduced or utilised in any form or by any electronic, mechanical, or other means, now known or hereafter invented, including photocopying and recording, or in any information storage or retrieval system, without permission in writing from the publishers.

Trademark notice: Product or corporate names may be trademarks or registered trademarks, and are used only for identification and explanation without intent to infringe.

British Library Cataloguing-in-Publication Data
A catalogue record for this book is available from the British Library

Library of Congress Cataloging-in-Publication Data
A catalog record for this book has been requested

ISBN: 978-1-138-82702-8 (hbk)
ISBN: 978-1-315-73879-6 (ebk)

Typeset in Bembo
by Apex CoVantage, LLC

My wife and I would like to dedicate this book to the memory of our late youngest son, Olughu Stephen Eliyas Okeke.

Contents

	List of figures	viii
	List of vignettes	ix
	Foreword	x
	Acknowledgements	xiv
1	Introduction: my search for an identity	1
2	The troubled birth of Nigeria: being an exile in my own land	21
3	Culture, identity and language: exploring my identity as a group analyst and Igbo man	33
4	The connections between language as one of our important cultural attributes and the development of identity	57
5	Talking to my peers: the importance of shared experiences	73
6	Analysis of and reflections on the group discussions	95
7	Two cultures, one identity: reflections on my attempts to bring together experiences from two conflicting cultures during my attempt to become an intercultural group psychotherapist	104
8	Bringing it all together: looking back, moving forward	139
	Index	153

Figures

1.1	The author, Okeke Azu-Okeke, on the occasion of his chieftaincy celebration, the final public ritual act for an Igbo man that can only be performed if the bird-shooting rite of passage has been fulfilled earlier in life	10
1.2	The daughter of the author carrying ceremonial smoked fish on the occasion of the author's chieftaincy celebration	11
1.3	The author and family on the occasion of his chieftaincy celebration	11
3.1	Cultural celebration of the marriage ritual: Breaking and sharing of kola nut and dry bush meat	51
3.2	Cultural celebration of the marriage ritual: Breaking and sharing of kola nut and dry bush meat	52
3.3	Funeral group	52
3.4	Funeral group	53
3.5	Funeral group	53
5.1	Members of age group of affiliation	80

Vignettes

1.1	Igba Nnunu, the bird-shooting rite of passage, and Ignu Nnunu, the celebration of the event	12
3.1	A chance encounter between a school teacher and her ex-pupil in a Nigerian market place	38
4.1	Reflections on beginning group analysis	61
7.1	Reflections on the impact of my training on kin relationships and country allegiance	112

Foreword

What does it feel like to be an exile in your own country? What does it feel like to be a child growing up in two very different cultures, trying to fit in and living in fear of 'breaking the rules' of one or both, most of the time? How does a child negotiate this complicated cultural context, develop and maintain his or her own identity in the face of overwhelming odds? What does it feel like to see one's precious objects – language, customs, religion – undermined and even destroyed?

I have been privileged and at the same time saddened to be present during Okeke's exploration of the above questions. His enquiries included exploring the effects of the colonial policies on all the different traditions and cultural beliefs in his own societies, and their freedom to practice these traditions and customs according to the norms that governed their existence and practices. As he points out, he began the research for this book with the premise that the effect of the British colonial ruling policies for all societies under the name of Nigeria was detrimental to the Igbo people in particular and all the other societies in general, and that it was affecting their personality, the sum total of their mental make-up as a people in their own right.

Yet, as time went on and his explorations deepened, he moved away from trying to prove his point through seeking only information that would support it. As a result he turned to a very wide selection of material including works from West African writers, policy documents, pamphlets and articles in the press, and perhaps most importantly, to seeking to understand how his fellow Igbos had experienced the impact of colonialism. He embarked on an ambitious task to obtain both written and spoken perspectives across generations, from the very few remaining elders (in the same age category as himself) to much younger people who had no direct experience of colonialism.

Though sometimes disappointed by the views of these younger people who, unlike himself and his older peers, could see only the benefits of colonialism, he took these on board and accepted that indeed there were some benefits, ironically one of these being the introduction of English as a compulsory language to be taught in schools, leading to writers being able to communicate to a much wider audience than before, and to a sense of unity developing across those very different societies that had been brought together under the name of 'Nigeria'. He accepted that the younger people tended to appreciate the material benefits of colonialism as they had not experienced the conflicts, nor the losses, of his own peer group. Nevertheless, he was determined that the history of this period of British colonialism should not be lost. It is very rare to find someone of Okeke's years, raised in 'Nigeria' under British colonial rule, who can make the kind of analysis that we find in this book. He describes his struggle of becoming a group analytic psychotherapist in a British training centre where he was the first and only Black student. Concepts that we might take for granted, such as the 'mind' and 'unconscious' have a completely different meaning or do not even exist in his own language and culture. So not only was he faced with being the only Black student he was struggling with very unfamiliar, alien ideas. In other words, he was faced again by a dominant ideology, that of Western psychoanalytic philosophy, which did not seek to respect and integrate the concepts from his Igbo culture in order to produce something new but took for granted that these had no place within the training's philosophy. Ironically, it did not seem to be anything extraordinary to the training centre to fail to take account of a Black person's social and cultural identity and how this might indeed contribute positively to the work! The question as to 'why are there so few Black psychotherapists in the UK', and especially Black psychoanalytic psychotherapists, is still being asked with as yet no real solution found. But perhaps it isn't so surprising given the still-present dominance of certain White European based values within psychoanalytic psychotherapy training and practice. Despite this issue being explored, pondered over and written about, taught and deeply felt by some psychotherapists and psychiatrists (White and Black), the situation that Roland Littlewood and Maurice Lipsedge wrote about in 1982, in *Aliens and Alienists*, a critique of the way that Black and minority ethnic patients were diagnosed with psychosis and over-represented in psychiatric services, still seems to prevail, at least in the UK. Pioneers – such as the late Jafar Kareem, a psychoanalyst who founded the Nafsiyat Intercultural Therapy Centre in 1983, and Suman Fernando, a psychiatrist who has made a powerful conceptual analysis of psychiatry and Western therapy and whose work lies in the tradition of the great psychiatrist and critic of colonialism Frantz Fanon – have drawn attention to the impact of racism on Black and Minority Ethnic Communities. Moodley and Ocampo (2014) in their edited work *Critical Psychiatry and Mental Health*, highlight the efforts of Fernando and his colleagues in trying to bring about changes in the psychological and psychiatric services to make them more culturally sensitive, pointing out that there is still a long way to go.

As Okeke rightly tells us, there are many pitfalls in attempting to produce a truly intercultural psychological therapy, as this would require immense knowledge and understanding of the socio-cultural context of all participants and willingness to embrace difference. Challenges to all participants, whatever their race, culture, class would be inevitable. That is hard enough when students shift into another; such has been the dominance of modality-led training in psychotherapy. I have heard psychotherapists from a psychoanalytic background (which is my own) expressing great anxiety about being 'disloyal' as they were asked to critically evaluate the theories that had formed the basis of their training. This situation is certainly changing, as the training for psychotherapy and counselling has moved into further and higher education, where a critical stance as opposed to an apprentice one is more the norm. But, following Kareem, Lipsedge, Littlewood, Fernando et al., we need to ask why there are still so few Black psychotherapists in the NHS and private practice when such a large percentage of clients are Black? If we move to considering psychotherapy services that might be useful for the vast number of refugees and migrants now living in Britain, we are faced with further challenges, not least in language and socio-cultural, religious backgrounds. At what stage might psychotherapy and counselling be helpful for people who have risked their lives to flee from war, experiencing the most horrific events, most probably traumatised and living a half-life in a country which may be ambivalent about their presence. Is it actually helpful at all? Who could provide a service to people in such a crisis – when just hearing what they have experienced is enough to cause the listener to feel helpless and distressed? Is there a danger that some services could make people already suffering feel worse?

Okeke's story reminds us that colonialism is still alive and well, even though British colonialism ended in West Africa many decades ago. The basis of colonialism, which is understood and well expressed by many of Okeke's participants, is the domination of one group over another. There are numerous examples of colonialism, past and present, throughout the world. The people subjected to colonialism may indeed experience benefits, such as improvements in infrastructure, opportunities through different and possibly more 'efficient' systems of governance, material benefits – and among Okeke's participants, it is the younger generation who are most aware of these. However, let's not forget that exploitation and destruction were and still are a major element in colonialism. Although it is unlikely that many of our clients will have had the experiences as described by Okeke, they are the heirs of them. Also, many we might encounter are likely to have fled their countries after escaping death from the results of power struggles elsewhere played out in their own countries – Syria and other parts of the Middle East being a case in point. What responsibility do we have to ensure that they are not going to experience another form of colonialism in the form of inappropriate social and psychiatric services when they try to settle and rebuild their lives as best they can, if they can? There are no answers in Okeke's book only very big and troubling questions for all of us, including those of us who try to be aware of world politics and their impact on our daily lives, and indeed our practice as psychotherapists. I am grateful to Okeke for enabling me at least to try and understand, through being present during his passionately described experiences, just what it might mean to witness your ways of life and that of your parents and elders denigrated and destroyed by an alien nation who purported to do all this 'for your own good' whilst obviously ruthlessly exploiting your country's resources and humiliating its people. The fact that he could use his conflicts, his confusion and anger and indeed his learning to make such an original contribution to the field of mental health and especially group analytic psychotherapy is our good fortune. Thank you, Okeke.

Professor Diane Waller

Diane Waller is Emeritus Professor of Art Psychotherapy at Goldsmiths, University of London, where she pioneered the training of Art Psychotherapists and developed a Master's degree in Group and Intercultural Therapy. She feels strongly that even now Black and Minority Ethnic groups are seriously under-represented in the psychotherapy profession. Having worked extensively in both East and Western Europe, helping to develop culturally relevant art therapy training, she now works part-time at the University of Brighton, Royal College of Art and Regent's University, supervising research students. In 2007, she was awarded an OBE for Services to Health.

Diane would like to thank Lorraine Slater for her invaluable help in putting the manuscript together and for her sensitivity in both copyediting and proofreading.

Reference list

Littlewood, R. and Lipsedge, M. (1982) *Aliens and Alienists*. London: Pelican Books.
Moodley, R. and Ocampo, M., eds. (2014) *Critical Psychiatry and Mental Health: Exploring the Work of Suman Fernando in Clinical Practice*. London and New York: Routledge.

Acknowledgements

The material for this book comes from research that I was primarily preparing for a PhD of Goldsmiths College, University of London. This process required the cooperation of various groups of people and individuals. These include members of different age groups of affiliations in my native Igboland who were kind enough to participate in group meetings in which we explored the effects of colonial rule in our particular areas in Nigeria. I am immensely grateful to these fellow citizens. I am also grateful to members of the Igbo Abiriba community here in the United Kingdom of Great Britain who made great efforts to respond to my questionnaires.

I am also immensely grateful to my supervisor Professor Diane Waller for her guidance and direction and her patience as I endeavoured to traverse through the journey of exploration of my cultural identity.

Finally, I am grateful to the late Dr. J. Stuart Whitely who gave me immense support and encouragement during my years of training and studies in psychotherapy and group analysis while working at the Henderson Therapeutic Community.

To all these people I say thank you.

Chapter 1

Introduction
My search for an identity

Introduction

This book will draw on my personal experience as an Igbo man of the older generation, growing up in two conflicting cultures: the traditional Igbo culture of Nigeria and that of the British colonialists. Though my story is the starting point, the journey is not only personal as I will make references to West African writers' views of colonialism and share the findings from interviews conducted with colleagues and friends of a similar age as well as those from other generations of Igbos. The book aims to contribute to a deeper awareness of the serious and particularly damaging aspects of colonialism, in whatever form it takes: the academic, the theoretical, the economic, and the psychological – which in ignoring deeply held social and spiritual values can alienate many trainees and potential clients from participating in the professions of psychotherapy and counselling. I will discuss my experience as the first and only Black Nigerian trainee in an Institute for Group Analysis in London and the impact this had on my future work as a lecturer and supervisor. Drawing on the learning from this time, I joined others, particularly staff and trainees of the Group and Intercultural Therapy programmes at Goldsmiths, University of London, in an effort to create a truly multicultural student community in which issues of 'difference' could be openly shared and in which a model of training could be co-created. The book will reflect on my research into traditional Igbo methods of healing and compare these with Western models, especially of group analysis, to see whether there is mutual learning to be achieved. It is informed by a qualitative, heuristic study using autoethnography, ethnography and narrative approaches, which I discuss further in Chapter Five. It is also informed by my experience as a mental health professional in radical NHS centres, such as the Henderson Hospital Surrey, the Aro hospital in Western Centre in Western Nigeria, and as a group analytic psychotherapist, teacher and supervisor. The book includes references to interviews with my peers in the older generation of Igbos in Nigeria and in London; on discussions with the younger generation, and on the writings of West African authors on the impact of colonialism. It also refers to official texts and analyses, and to documents of colonial times which demonstrate how the policies of colonialism affected every aspect of life – family life, religious practices, economics, administration – driven by a wish to destroy these and replace them with a set of values that were alien to the colonised people.

The search for identity and meaning in the face of deep cultural conflicts will be significant in a time of mass migration either for economic, social or political reasons. Although the book focuses on British Colonialism in Nigeria, the effects of colonialism in other settings are very much present today in other societies and therefore can be generalised to other populations.

There is still relatively little literature that explores intercultural aspects of psychotherapy in terms of training and treatment or that asks questions about the still very few Black psychotherapists, while there is an over-representation of Black clients in mental health. Despite the work of Littlewood and Lipsedge (1982) and a few authors who have raised concerns about racism within psychotherapy and counselling (e.g., Farhad Dalal, Isha McKenzie-Mavinga) and in psychiatry (Suman Fernando), there are still no texts that incorporate actual experience of colonialism, racism and the impact of this on the life and work of a group.

In this chapter, I will discuss the following issues to which I will return throughout the book:

1 British Colonialism in our West African societies that the colonialists' named 'Nigeria'.
2 The exilic social condition of life lived by the author under colonialism.
3 The threat to the attainment of my social identity by the process of performing a customary and traditional rite of passage.
4 The aim of the book in the light of the above factors.

British colonialism in our West African societies

I will begin with a brief description of what came to be called the country of 'Nigeria' as this is the context for the book. 'Nigeria' is made up of many different societies with independent cultures and histories – the principal ones being the Hausas, the Igbos, and the Yorubas. It is the largest 'country' in Africa with a population of about 20,469,047 according to one 2016 censor. (Understandably, different censors give different figures of the population.) Between 45% to 50% of the population are Christians, most of whom live in the southern region. The earliest known documentation of Nigeria is that it was the site of a group of organised states called Hausa. The earliest Nigerians were skilled artisans known as the Noks. By the second millennium they had disappeared and since then, successions of groups of people have inhabited and established kingdoms in these geographical areas. By the 1300s the empire of Kanem-Bornu was flourishing as a centre of Islamic culture rivalling Mali in the West. By the late 16th century, the Kanem-Bornu broke up and the Hausa states regained their independence. In the 19th century, the Fulani then took dominance in the lands of the Hausas. The southern part of the country was divided into the Yoruba states in the South West while the Edos ruled in Binin in the south central parts and the Igbos had control of the East and in the North of the Niger delta.

European explorers such as Mungo Park, Richard Lemon Lander and John Lander first explored the interior in 1830–31. Realising the potential of the territories, the Portuguese, the British and others established slave trading stations in the Niger delta. The British sent consuls to the riverine territories Calabar and Lagos where trading posts were established and the colonialists took full possession of Lagos.

The British colonialists then established protectorates after the conclusions of several treaties with the native chiefs. In 1893, the name Niger Coast Protectorates was established.

In 1900 after expansion in the south west, which brought about the addition of the kingdom of Benin, the name was changed to the protectorate of Southern Nigeria. In the same year, the British proclaimed the protectorate of Northern Nigeria as well. They did not have full control over either of the two protectorates at the time of their establishments.

France, Britain and Germany had spheres of influence in Nigeria of which Britain had the control. British troops were engaged in any such conflicts as arose with the native people who were still involved in the slave trade after it was prohibited by the British in 1807.

In 1914, North and South Nigeria merged into what was then called the colony and protectorate of Nigeria with Sir Frederick Lugard as the governor. However, for administrative purposes, the country was divided into the Colony of Lagos, Northern province and Southern province. Lugard allowed the native chiefs and councils to rule over Nigeria under the watchful eyes of the British government.

In reality, then, what is called the country of 'Nigeria' consists of various autonomous societies of culturally and historically independent nations whose integrity and social status remained indelible in their psyche. Their status as part of a united country called 'Nigeria' is elusive and in reality it is only a fantasy and an illusion.

This then is the background to my Igbo society and the other societies that jointly came to be called 'Nigeria'. It is important that I emphasise this context, as my experiences of life within it (during the occupation and after the British colonisers left) have raised more questions in my mind about myself, my identity, than I have answers. Hence I undertake to go on this journey of exploration in anticipation of finding some answers to those questions.

For much of my adult life and particularly since undertaking training in Group Analytic Psychotherapy at the Institute of Group Analysis, London between 1988 and 1993, I have been preoccupied with the question: what happens to the identity of the person who is raised in one culture but who then comes to feel and find himself an 'exile' in his own land because of the impact of colonialism on his life?

Furthermore what is the impact of colonialism on the people of the colonised land who are faced with the denigration of dearly held traditions and overt racism?

I am aware that many authors have addressed colonialism from different perspectives, and I will refer to them later. My priority in this book will be, however, to make an original contribution to knowledge in the field of psychotherapy and in particular, group analysis. This claim is based on the following:

a   To my knowledge after investigation, I have not found any account in the literature of group analysis that is written from the perspective of a group analyst who is himself a product of a colonised society.
b   Though some authors (notably the late Professor Ian Craib at the University of Essex) combined sociological-political insights with group analysis, and Raman Kapur and Jim Campbell (2004) addressed the 'Troubles' in Northern Ireland from a psychoanalytic-political perspective, they did not address colonialism.

Other authors such as Frantz Fanon (2001) have addressed racism within psychoanalytic theory but have not in my view done so from a similar position as my own. D'Ardenne and Mahtani (2008) first addressed 'transcultural counselling' in 1989 and their book has been revised and reprinted 12 times, indicating the need for therapists to 'recognise the importance of life experiences for their work, and to think about ways of using their own skills and resources more flexibly in response to different cultural needs'. Farhad Dalal (2002), a Group Analyst, produced a new theory of racism based on group analytic theory; Frank Lowe (2014) edited *Thinking Space: Promoting thinking about Race, Culture and Diversity in Psychotherapy and Beyond*; Roy Moodley and Martha Ocampo (2014) wrote *Critical Psychiatry and Mental Health, exploring the work of Suman Fernando in Clinical Practice*; and Roy Moodley, Uwe Gielen and Rosa Wu (2013) wrote *Handbook of Counselling and Psychotherapy in an International Context* in which there are two chapters concerning counselling and psychotherapy in West Africa and Nigeria relevant to this book. (Lonzozou Kpanake and Omar Ndoye, 'Counselling and Psychotherapy in Francophone West Africa: Creating a future vision'; and Olaniyi Bojuwoye and Andrew A. Mogaji, 'Counselling and Psychotherapy in Nigeria: Horizons for the future'). The Journals *Therapy Today* and *New Associations* have featured interviews with prominent practitioners of psychotherapy and counselling (e.g., Isha McKenzie-Mavinga, 'Racism in Counselling and Psychotherapy', *Therapy Today*, Vol 25, 3, 2014; and 'Silenced: The Black student experience', *Therapy Today*, Vol. 24, 10, 2013, an interview in which Eugene Ellis, an integrative art psychotherapist and founder of the Black and Asian Therapists' Network discussed how group processes can often be very difficult for some Black students in a predominately White trainee group). We see that the issues that I shall raise in my book are far from being resolved and indeed the issue of racism in psychotherapy and counselling is alive and well.

c The first and only Master's level programme in the UK to address Intercultural Therapy, with emphasis on the very racially and culturally mixed trainees' personal experiences, including racism, started at University College, London, followed by a practical and theoretical training at Goldsmiths in 1994, building on the Postgraduate Diploma in Group Psychotherapy (1988–2010) that had the stated aim of achieving a 'truly multicultural community of trainees'. By 2010, both these programmes had closed (ostensibly for financial reasons), leaving a very big gap in training, and the status quo of psychotherapy trainees and practitioners being predominately white continues. This fact is acknowledged in recent issues of *The Psychotherapist* (United Kingdom Council for Psychotherapy) (2015), and the *Psychoanalytic Psychotherapy Newsletter* (2012). My research will of necessity examine my own contributions; clearly through having completed all my higher education and professional training in the United Kingdom I have had to work hard to integrate or perhaps more accurately 'live with' two very different socio-cultural perspectives. My own story has to be the starting point, but the journey is not only a personal one, as I shall demonstrate through references to African writers and through interviews with colleagues and friends who are of a similar age and those from other generations. [(See vignettes 1.1, 3.1, 4.1, 7.1)].

d Thus the combination of the above will, I hope, contribute to a deeper awareness of the serious and particularly damaging aspects of colonialism, in whatever form – that is the academic, theoretical and economic – on the people we see. The lack of such appreciation within my own profession of psychotherapy is particularly surprising, given we are in the United Kingdom, a multicultural society.

e I shall use the findings of my research to discuss traditional Igbo methods of healing and compare with Western models, especially of group analysis, to see whether there is mutual learning to be achieved.

f I shall use 'we' and 'us' throughout to identify myself with my origin as an Igbo man and the community in which I grew up.

The exilic social conditions of living that our colonised societies endured under colonialism

At the time that I was born, according to our traditional system of determining periods and times of important events such as birth and death, the colonial powers were already occupying our societies. This means that as my eyes opened to see the world that I was living in, it was a world that was struggling to deal with some difficult social conditions, the cause of which eluded me during the early parts of my life. But the aura of the alien culture brought about by strange people in the vicinities of my immediate society was inescapable. Even before I saw the first white person in my life, I heard different stories about this breed of human beings.

So as I was growing up, it was in an atmosphere filled with whispers of how we used to be, how we now were and speculations about what we might become. The seed of uncertainty had been sown in my mind. This is how it came to be that right from the beginning of my life the circumstances of my life were already compromised by the presence of the alien culture of the British colonialists; this presence especially clearly militated against our native traditional cultures.

I will now discuss the factor of the exilic social conditions of living that members of our societies, including the author, endured under colonialism.

The Rabbi of Belz, Shalom ben Elazar Rokeach of the 19th century, addressing the situation of Jews, wrote that there are three types of exiles. The first is when Jews are in exile among other nations. The second is when Jews are in exile among other Jews. And the third is when a Jew is exiled within himself. This, he considers to be the hardest of all to endure.

To these, however, I would add the exile that a people suffer within their own native lands. That is, being in social and emotional conditions of living that were comparable to those of people who were forced to leave their homeland to move to a new and strange one because they are denied the freedom that they need to practise their cultural traditions and customs. We were thereby denied our right to celebrate and enjoy our ways of life. We were also denied freedom of worship according to our religious traditions and thereby barred from developing and maintaining our own desires for our present life and for posterity as a people in our own right.

By the use of political, economic and military forces, the colonialists coerced, and subjected us, the Igbo people, and all other members of our societies to the social conditions of people living as if in exile away from our own native land. I would argue that this is the most dehumanising and degrading form of social relationship that I can imagine. It was degrading to us as we, the affected people, found it difficult to live our lives in the ways that we felt we should – that is, the ways that our ancestors had done and we had been brought up to do, and our descendants would have been brought up to do. These ways were our customary ways that had come down to us from time immemorial. This statement should not be seen as suggesting that we reject change when we find it necessary to adjust any aspects of our ways of life. Planning and making any changes are quite acceptable to us as we are well aware that no position in life is permanent. In order to know where to make changes in our lives, it is necessary that we understand the life that we are living so that we would know where that can lead us to. The collective free will to carry out any changes in our ways of life and living must be distinguished from having any type of life changes thrust on us unilaterally, especially changes that proved to militate against our welfare including our future prospects.

It was precisely because these conditions were forced on us that they were so degrading and so humiliating in the sense that having such changes forced on us made us to feel infantilised, immature and childlike. We felt robbed of our reasoning capacities, as if we had not after all been living as people with their own tried and tested social order. It was as if how we had lived our lives was after all inappropriate, including the cultural institutions and the traditions we had developed before the colonialists forced themselves into our societies and our lives.

I would argue that this amounted to nothing less than coercion made possible by threats of the use of military and economic forces. Coercion means the use of force to make someone or people to do something. If, as was the case, we were forced to do things in the ways that our colonisers wanted us to do them, it is obvious that we were being asked to do what we did not want to do. We were not allowed our freedom to do things in the way that we were accustomed to doing them.

This was particularly the case with regard to those things which conflicted with the interest of our colonisers. Our freedom in our own societies was denied to us. It felt as I believe it would have felt to people who were exiled from their own homelands. Although we were in our own homelands we were denied access to our cultural heritage. The British colonisers of our societies were well aware of these conflicting cultures, but they did not feel that their policies that had brought these types of approach were either coercive or dehumanising. Rather they argued that what we experienced as being coerced into were actions we would have done for ourselves if we had known better.

This brings to mind what Sir Isaiah Berlin (1959) said in his inaugural lecture to Oxford university in 1958 by the title of 'Two concepts of liberty'. Berlin distinguished between two concepts or forms of liberty (freedom) – negative liberty and positive liberty and argued that the concept of positive liberty had often been used to cover up abuse leading to curtailment of people's negative liberties 'for their own good'. Berlin believed that positive liberty nearly always gave rise to abuse of power. For example, when a political leadership like the British colonialists realised that they had the means both military and economic to exploit our natural and human resources to their advantage, they invoked the ideology of positive liberty to justify their policies of dislocation and rupturing of our cultural institutions for their own good.

I would argue strongly that we remain in illusion about who we, as Igbos, really are in relation to other people of the world. Some of the consequences of the application of the positive/negative ideology to our social conditions, such as the attitudes of the Black Victorians that I will discuss briefly later, have exacerbated bringing about the culture of Couriferism (see Chapters Two and Three). Our saving grace, however, is that we retain the consciousness that we belong somewhere other than where we find ourselves in our relationships with the British colonialists, wandering in our illusions as if we were in a haze. Most often we live in a dream world created by the conflicts between our entrenched primordial cultural heritage and the intruding alien culture of the colonialists pressing to displace this. We do not have to hold that which is ours because we have been separated from it, and that which is dangled in front of us as the alternative in the form of the colonialists' cultural values are for us difficult to hold on to because they were never meant for us. Not even the colonialists who passed them to us as our legacy believed that they would suit our way of life.

It is from those of our citizens in whose psyche our culture was so strongly entrenched that our salvation from the position of total eradication of our cultural heritage from our consciousness came. Through their power to enter imaginatively into the minds of our native characters whose behaviours mirrored our cultural practices and traditions, the West African novelists were able to present these reflections in the mirrors of our cultural traditions to the readers of our societies. Thereby our true culture and traditions that had evolved over centuries (our heritage) were kept in our consciousness against the background of the effects of colonial policies that were militating against them. By playing out in his writing different versions of our traditional village lives through his characters, Chinua Achebe, the West African novelist, kept our traditions and cultural practices alive in our consciousness.

I believe that it was this state and type of relationship that existed between us and our colonisers that prompted Frantz Fanon, as he analysed the relationship between the Black man under colonial rule, to say that the shadow of colonised man splits his presence and distorts his outline, breaches his boundaries, repeats his action at a distance, disturbs and divides the very time of his being. According to this assessment by Fanon, the presence of the White man has adverse effects on the Black man in many ways. The presence of the White people with the Black people of our societies gave rise to what Fanon referred to as 'a certain sensitising action'. According to Fanon, if his psychic structure is weak, the Black man experiences a collapse of his ego.

In effect the Black man projects his super ego to the White man as superior to him. He ceases to be proactive and withdraws from taking actions independently as he concentrates his attentions on the idealised White man on whose evaluations the Black man believes rests the criteria for evaluating his own self-worth and self-esteem.

The degree to which we were or were not able to adapt to the new and different ways of life was a function of the extent to which we were or were not able to resist these disorganising and confusing experiences of life under the colonial regime. It was also the function of the strength of our entrenched cultural traditions within our psyche.

Here again emotions arouse the rueful Igbos lamentations of 'M*a obughu nwa beke Igbo mara ihegha ge me*', meaning, 'If it were not for the White man's interventions, we, the Igbos, know what we can do'. Put in another way, we know our capability.

In one sense this is an admission of being in a state of impotence to fight against the social injustices of the White man as well as our consciousness of who we are in terms of our heritage, in spite of the pressure on us to turn our backs on it.

This is the social condition that I had to endure, hence my consciousness of a threat to my attaining an important social status that can only be achieved by performing an important rite of passage, which I will now discuss.

The threat to my (the author's) attainment of my social status and identity by performing the customary traditional rite of passage

The nature of our Igbo social traditions and my belonging also to the Christian religion, placed me in a state of cross-cultural conflict and often great anxiety about the danger of not being able to attain my obligatory status of '*onye gbala Nnunu*' – he who has shot a bird – followed by the ritual celebrations of that feat, namely *Ignu Nnunu*. This ceremony is an important rite of passage with great significance in the developmental processes of the young males of the society. The obligation of every young male of the society within a certain age range is to demonstrate his archery skill by shooting a bird in the forest with his bow and arrow.

I feared that I would be exposed to shame and ridicule if, for any reason other than severe deformity, I did not perform the rite. It would also mean that by such default I would break the link in the chain of the social order of the society. On the other hand if I performed this rite, as a Christian widely known and referred to by my fellow citizens as 'Onye Chochi – 'Church person or Christian' – I would be considered by my fellow Christians to be a heathen if the ritual was deemed by the Christian tradition as contrary to Christian doctrines. This was an important issue about which I felt that I had to have my parents' guidance and support on the correct course of action.

Celebration of this rite was very crucial to my future position in the society and to my status within my age group of affiliation. Anyone who failed, and even today anyone who fails to perform this rite within the designated age range, would suffer the indignity of derision from within his group and outside it. Because of the general belief in the integrity of the rite and its function in the social order of the society, it commands wide interest mainly on its altruistic value but also on its psychological significance to the ego development of the male children of this culture. Each rite of passage marks a developmental stage in the life of a male person.

The taunts for failing to perform this rite never go away completely until the debt that it represents is paid. It remains in people's memory only to surface again and again, as it is invoked as a demon whenever individuals or groups are reminded of it by circumstances. For example, a defaulter will not be given

Figure 1.1 The author, Okeke Azu-Okeke, on the occasion of his chieftaincy celebration, the final public ritual act for an Igbo man that can only be performed if the bird-shooting rite of passage has been fulfilled earlier in life

Figure 1.2 The daughter of the author carrying ceremonial smoked fish on the occasion of the author's chieftaincy celebration

Figure 1.3 The author and family on the occasion of his chieftaincy celebration

the right to traditional marriage rite ceremonies if, by that stage in his life, he has not performed the rite. It is not easy for it to escape being remembered that someone had committed such act of omission in his social obligations in a close-knit society where its celebration involves a wide cross-section of that society. The celebration involves members of the celebrant's age group and people of different age groups and gender who, if it ever became a debatable issue, would bear witness according to their memory that the event was celebrated.

This is especially so in a society in which historical events are transmitted through the characteristic means of oral tradition, the recall of memory and the transmission of such memory by word of mouth.

There was and indeed there is no way of escaping the performance of this rite or indeed any other rite of passage. There is no escaping the form of social and moral sanctions that are exacted from the delinquent citizen as retribution. In reality, people usually perform this rite, even if it means doing so at a later age in their lives. This is to avoid the stigma attached to defaulting in the performance and in order to avoid being denied the privilege of the ultimate social honour when this is due at the later part of their lives – that is, the time of performing the 'Uche' chieftaincy ceremonial rites, the final public ritual act for a male member of the Abiriba Igbo society, after which he retires from all active public social duties.

The likelihood that I might be prevented from or handicapped in the performance of this rite haunted me for a long time. Each time that I went out with my friends to hunt birds with my bow and arrows, I was affected by anxiety on two levels. On one level it was about having the opportunity and the skill required to shoot down a bird with my bow and arrow. It is not an easy skill to master. My other anxiety was an ideological one, namely a concern that the eldest son of an Elder in a Christian church might not be allowed to perform this traditional cultural rite of passage.

Vignette 1.1 Igba Nnunu, the bird-shooting rite of passage, and Ignu Nnunu, the celebration of the event

The day of reckoning as it were, did come for me for this land mark event of my life, on which I performed the 'Igba Nnunu' – shooting of the bird – and the accompanying 'Ignu Nnunu', celebration of the shoot.

On that day I was filled with a sense of great achievement but within me I knew that all could prove to be meaningless if because I was a Christian I was forbidden by my Christian principles from performing the ceremonial rite, the most important part of this rite of passage. My friends and I hurried to get home from the forest, full of excitement and anticipation.

My father was not at home when I arrived at our house with my bird followed by my friends all of us feeling jubilant, triumphant and proud that I had 'shot my bird'. But all of us were also aware that we had won only half the battle. It would have been of no significance to me or to any one else for that matter if my father came home and told me that I could not be allowed to celebrate this important traditional rite because it was considered to contradict with Christian traditions.

So my friends and I waited for my father to get home so that I could ask him to guide me on what I could or could not do in this situation of potential cross-cultural issue affecting my social life. As we waited, it seemed as if we had been waiting for ages, when we saw my father in the distance, approaching. My friends, most of who were themselves non-Christians but were still loyal and sympathetic to my belief, nudged me. I moved forward towards my father as he stopped in front of us. I believe that he suspected that I had something important to talk to him about. I told him that I had shot my traditional ritual 'bird' and wanted to know whether as a Christian I could perform the ceremonial rite of 'Ignu Nnunu'. My father paused for a moment. I felt that he was impressed by the fact that I had the presence of mind to wait for him and ask him for guidance. He told me to wait where I stood with my friends, and then left us and went to the next compound where his fellow Elder of the church of the Scotland Mission lived. It was obvious to me that he had gone to consult with him about this important issue. It seemed like ages as we waited for my father to return. Then he did with the best news that I had ever heard in my life up till that time and news that has made a lasting impact in my life. My father told me that it was alright for me to go and celebrate the victory, of my prowess. My friends and I could hardly contain our joy and jubilation. I considered it to be a great victory for our cultural traditions, for Christian tradition and for my own authenticity as a young Abiriba Igbo man who had achieved a higher social status in my society by the performance of this rite of passage. The next stage of this great event was then to follow.

Having been prepared by my father for the celebration by being decorated with a copper ring round my waist and a string of cowry beads round my neck, I set out with my friends.

We went from one relative to the other so that they would all bear witness with great pride to this great achievement of their young relative. In acknowledgement and respect of this event we were presented with gifts of money, yams, corn cobs and kola nuts and dry bush meat. The appreciation of this feat of heroism was expressed by the members of the society who saw me and my entourage as we went along celebrating this conquest. By their expressions older men showed that they remembered their time with as much pride as I was doing as the man of the moment.

They cheered me with as much enthusiasm as the younger ones who became more energised and determined to shoot their bird and perform this rite of passage did.

I was frequently challenged to recount my experiences of this adventure in the customary way by the challenger calling out; 'Eti, bia bai rim' are the operative words by which the young warrior is obliged to run forward to the challenger or challengers and recount his adventure. It is a challenge which when seriously made is not to be ignored but taken seriously. Otherwise it might be thought that the celebrant did not fight the battle of skill and tact which were instrumental to his conquest. Accordingly on hearing those words I would hasten to the challenger and recount the processes that led to my conquest by saying the appropriate battle words which every victorious warrior must know.

As he arrives to a close proximity of the challenger or challengers, he greets him or them by saying, 'Mma ma nu. Anom uluo ikwuru ya bia bei. Mgbaya, ya dapusa. Mnwuru ya'.

This translated into the English language says: 'I was in the bush hut when it (the bird) came, I shot it down and caught it'.

As if to relate to the brave hunter's experience of the throes of war and to acknowledge the hardship as an inevitable price of victory, the challenger identifies with this hardship by sprinkling sand on the young hunter's head. Each time that he is called upon he obliges by going through the process of narrating his experience of the great event. And each time he endeavours to do so with equal air of the seriousness of the event and the occasion.

I went round with my entourage until we felt that we had done enough and as many people as possible had seen me and my group and we were also too tired to continue. We decided to go home and shared our gifts among ourselves. We had at the end of all this by following the traditions ensured that my conquest had become public knowledge. By so doing we had ensured also that there would always be some people still alive in the foreseeable future who can testify to this event having taken place especially since our society is an oral traditional cultural society which does not customarily keep written records of events.

The brave hunter's greatest reward is usually the success in achieving this great feat in his life. It usually raises his social status in his community. He is usually sufficiently satisfied with that social achievement that he does not object to the older and loyal friends in the group taking larger share of the gifts that they had received.

There is a significant reason for publicly celebrating this rite of passage. In a society of oral traditional culture in which traditions are transmitted by words of mouth, important events such as this are best marked by exposure to the public gaze of young and old and as many as are available to witness it.

If the early rite of passage is omitted, this usually has implications for the individual's personal dignity in the society as people talk about such things. There is an implication for his social standing, starting with the dignity of his age group of affiliation. The individual who in an older age group has not fulfilled this rite of passage is deemed to represent a source of shame to the whole of his age group of affiliation. Since age groups at higher levels observe their social rituals at the same calendar time, there are usually people within each age group who may cast a shadow to dim the bright light of the achievements of the whole group and blight their moments of glory.

These considerations are usually taken so seriously by the whole group that they would decide to recover their pride as a group by undertaking to help their comrade to fulfil this social obligation. This may be by helping him to shoot a bird, even at such late period in his social life, and supporting him emotionally through the celebratory part of the ritual. In the event of lateness in performing this rite of passage there may be possible stigma as a result. For that reason a large number of the members of his age group would take away some of the focus of attention on him by helping him in the areas of his difficulties in achieving this objective. In my particular circumstances, I was relieved, proud and happy to have accomplished this social event. It meant to me and my friends that colonial rule had not disrupted this very significant cultural heritage and left me bereft of my identity as an Abiriba man of the Igbo nation, and for that I feel triumphant.

At the same time, I have resented the fact that I had been forced by foreign cultural traditions that had no respect for my own, to go through experiences of emotional conflicts over my legitimate right to perform my traditional cultural rites.

I have also come to resent the denigration of some of our philosophy for the healing of illnesses by the colonialists which to me in particular means another rejection of what we the Igbo 'Nigerians' believe in and hold dear.

The aims of the book

Having described the context of the book and some of the challenges I faced on embarking on this story, the reader needs to know that my primary aim is to respond to my inner feelings as an Abiriba man of the Igbo nation arising from my experiences of colonial rule over our societies from my formative years. As now an 'elder' of the Igbo nation and a long-term practising group psychotherapist, I hope that my story will encourage others to reflect on and perhaps to approach with more insight those citizens who, like me, have grown up within two conflicting cultures, been subject to racism and denigration of their culture and society, and had to struggle to accept themselves and establish a place where their specific experience could be valued and indeed useful. My experiences left me confused about my identity as I have stated earlier. That was until I read in Mang E. Obasi (2003) what was reportedly published in The

Manchester Guardian Weekly of Thursday October 10, 1957, under the title 'Two Faces of Ghana', and it read:

> The young men of Ghana cannot often tell you the origin of the Golden Stool of Ashanti, nor will they willingly discuss their own tribal stories of inheritance, but they are often embarrassingly well informed about the house of Tudor and sometimes quoted Joshua or Leviticus with quite disconcerting accuracy.

This report makes similar reading to what a documented version of my own experiences of the outcome of the British colonialists' curricula for our education in our colonised societies would read like. It brought back to me memories of my alienation from my cultural education, which was treated as not conforming to the type of education suitable to prepare us for our future life in the wider and more civilised world communities.

One of our great African statesmen Jomo Kenyatta (1979) was also quoted as saying:

> To Moigoi and Wamboi and all the disposed youth of Africa: for perpetuation of communion with ancestral spirit through the fight for African freedom, and in the firm faith that the dead, the living and the unborn will unite to rebuild the destroyed shrine.

The emphasis was on rebuilding the destroyed shrine; this was what Jomo Kenyatta was calling on the youths of Africa to awaken to. Earlier in this chapter, I lamented the destructions of our shrines of the spirits of our ancestors, both metaphorically and practically in physical terms. I feel that my own spirit of nationalism and sense of responsibility to my traditional cultural heritage were stirred by the above statement by Jomo Kenyatta.

The statement brought back my memory of how the British colonial policies were so cruelly applied to our societies that we became subjugated to a point of helplessly acquiescing to all the British colonial values to the detriments of our traditional cultural heritage, our nationhood.

More voices of persuasion came from Isichei (1976) who expressed his view on this saying that 'People will not look forward to posterity who never look backwards to their ancestors'. Ejiofor (1984), writing about cultural revival in Igboland, cited President Leopold Senghor of Senegal who in 1977 expressed his opinion on the importance of our culture to our future as a people in similar tone of voice saying that no problem is more important for Black people than that of culture.

A common link to all these statements is the one firm and indefatigable belief that these nationalists hold that people's culture and their history form the backbone of any hope which they might entertain of having a future. People's culture and their history hold for them the faith and pride that can carry them to the height of power and survival.

We were coerced to accept that the shrines of our ancestors were valueless and fit only to be consigned to the dust bin in the hierarchy of religious Darwinism. By shrine I am not referring only to the symbolic iconic objects of our worship. I am referring most particularly to our inner spirit which is attached to our being and our heritage and which animates our doyen nationalists such as Kenyatta. Our younger nationalists who, through their writings and through their public speeches, keep alive in us our consciousness of our cultural heritage, which we were otherwise increasingly at the risk of losing due to our intellectual lethargy and stupor fermented by the sufferings from humiliations, subjugations and dejections orchestrated by the British colonialists.

We were in danger of becoming drowned in the effects of these subjugations and degradations, with the consequence of relapsing to the point of disconnectedness from those attributes that say who we are as a people, the attributes which mirror our cultural origin. That was the stage in our lives when we no longer knew where we were going because unless we knew where we were coming from, we could not know where to advance towards as our future.

That is why we must know our past and never forget it, otherwise, our unknown past will, like unlaid ghosts, continue to hinder our progress to the future until we regain our awareness of what they are. He who does not know from where he is coming cannot know where he is really going.

I believe that that is the reason why I felt the inner compulsion to examine the dual life that colonialism had made me to lead today and that I also believe most of our Igbo population leads.

That is why I believe that it is of paramount importance that we understand the full impact of the relationship that our British colonisers created and had with us, so that we will be able to regain our orientations of where we have come from and have some strategies for engaging with the future. This is not a matter of measuring our, the colonised people's, traditional cultures against those of our colonisers. It is simply that we seem to have stagnated and become incapable of progressing and advancing into more successful societies in the world community.

We have only succeeded in getting trapped between the two worlds of the cultures of our colonisers and ourselves because of the legacies that our colonisers bequeathed to us. Through the types of relationships that they created through their ruling policies, they steeped us into the lethargy and stupor where we have remained, stagnated in the euphoria of an elusive unity of a place named the country of Nigeria.

Given the very difficult and inhumane experiences of our life under the colonial rule, it is not surprising that there were many in our societies who hoped and prayed for a time of deliverance from the exilic lifestyle that was imposed on us. We prayed for the time of our freedom to come and indeed that time came when, on the first of October 1960, we were declared to be an independent country from the British government.

There was much hope and jubilation that our life as people was going to change for the better. Some of what we thought were signs of hope proved to be generators of experiences of euphoria, a false sense that we now had the opportunity of enjoying the kind of comfort of our colonisers. We had been angry and frustrated by our humiliations at the hands of the British colonisers as we watched them from some distance in our communities. Now that they had departed, we were confronted with a different kind of reality: that is, the realisation that we did not have the creative know-how to produce the kind of comfort and lifestyles that we begrudged the colonisers of having at our expense. Because it was always part of our colonisers' plans to keep from us such strategic knowledge and planning skills that would enable us to compete with them.

To compound this disappointment we had lost most of our own skills for applying our own traditional political system. Our elders and culture-carriers who were sidelined and whose powers of governing their people were greatly denigrated by the colonialists had died away with the passage of time of the colonial rule. Those who were left in positions of some authority were subject to the guidelines of the colonialists' regulations. The powers of our traditional rulers were no longer guided by those principles which were embodied in our oral traditional culture. They were no longer guided by those principles by which all the important aspects of our cultural life were protected and in which our religious sentiments and conformity with our social norms took high priority.

Another factor at play in the difficulties that had followed us virtually into this state of neo-colonialism is our colonialists' legacy to us of an illusion of a united country. In many ways, the only thing which is certain about Nigeria as a country of all the different societies that are included in that name, is the fact that it is not united. The fact that this is the case is not due to lack of efforts by the colonialists to forge such a country as is evident in the fact that such an idea had already moved from them thinking about it to putting it into practice in the form of their unilateral declaration of it. That at the very least was in the hope that it might become a reality.

If, for instance, the amalgamated societies became a united country in real sense, the colonialists would have pointed to the magnitude of their political wisdom. That did not materialise, but they nevertheless used the idea and the illusion that it created for the furtherance of their advantage, in the realisation of their economic ambitions of acquisition of our natural resources. Hence in the final analysis it was for the colonialists – heads they won, and tails we, the colonised people, lost.

In this book I will discuss the events in all the societies which were grouped together by our colonisers and named the country of 'Nigeria' during the period in the nineteenth to twentieth century between 1880 and 1914.

This was when most of the world outside Europe and America was formally partitioned into territories under the formal rule or informal political dominations of one or the other of the few imperialist states in Europe and America. Britain was one of these and colonised the West African societies that they came to name 'Nigeria'.

I will show that their ruling policies culminated in the rupture and dislocations of our societies' institutions and cultural traditions. The effective outcome of this for us was our loss of our civil, political, economic and human rights as a people. The nature of these losses included restriction of our freedom to exercise our human rights and to freely plan our future and satisfy our needs according to our customs and aspirations, using our own natural resources.

I argue that in the process of this relationship we have become effectively psychically colonised and, as a consequence, we have projected our super egos onto our colonisers. With the loss of control of our psychic life, we could no longer direct and guide our children to develop the impetus for organising their identity since development of identity is a function of our culture. That is a function of our roots from which the structure and organisation of our identity develops

Hence another major aim is to highlight these effects of the British colonial policies on the Igbo people in particular, and on all other societies included in the country named as Nigeria, namely loss of confidence on our own national identity and our self-worth as human beings.

However, this book does not aim to be merely plaintiff about the circumstances of the British colonisation of our societies or even of the fact that our societies were colonised. The author recognises that there are historical evidences to show that Britain itself was at some historical periods in time colonised and suffered the adverse consequences of that.

To advance my arguments I will draw from the following sources:

- My own experiences of life during the colonisation period and since after the occupation of our societies by the British colonialists.
- The views and testimonies of individuals and groups in our societies, their experiences of the colonial periods in our societies and on their views about the colonial legacies left to us.
- The contributions of the West African novelists and writers who through literary work revealed their awareness of the adverse effects that the colonial policies were having on us and had continued to have on our societies. They proceeded to alert the rest of the members of our societies and of the dangers of ignoring these adverse effects.
- The benefit of the author's own training and clinical practice experience as a group analyst, to analyse the effects of the colonial policies on the Igbo people and thus to contribute to greater understanding of how these policies affected subsequent generations, including those living in the UK.

I will now discuss some of the measures that we were obliged to adopt to deal with the social conditions that we found ourselves in because of colonialism in our West African societies.

Reference list

Abolition of the Slave Trade Act 1807. Parliament of the United Kingdom.
Berlin, I. (1959) *Two Concepts of Liberty*. Oxford: Clarendon Press.
Dalal, F. (2002) *Race, Colour and the Processes of Racialization*. London and New York: Routledge.
d'Ardenne, P. and Mahtani, A. (2008) *Transcultural Counselling in Action*. London: SAGE.
Ejiofor, P.N.O. (1984) *Cultural Revival in Igboland*. Onitsha: University Publishing Company.
Ellis, E. (2013) 'Silenced: The Black student experience', *Therapy Today*, 24(10).
Fanon, F. (2001) *The Wretched of the Earth: Psychoanalytic Theory of Racism*. London: Penguin Classics.
Isichei, E. (1976) *History of the Igbo People*. London: Macmillan.
Kapur, R. and Campbell, J. (2004) *The Troubled Mind of Northern Ireland: An Analysis of the Emotional Effect of the Troubles*. London: Karnac books.
Kenyatta, J. (1979) *Facing Mount Kenya*. London: Heinemann.
Littlewood, R. and Lipsedge M. (1982) *Aliens and Alienists: Ethnic Minorities and Psychiatry*. London: Penguin.
Lowe, F., ed. (2014) *Thinking Space: Promoting Thinking About Race, Culture and Diversity in Psychotherapy and Beyond*. Tavistock Clinic Series. London: Karnac.
McKenzie-Mavinga, I. (2014) 'Racism in counselling and psychotherapy', *Therapy Today*, 25(3).
Moodley, R. and Ocampo, M., eds. (2014) *Critical Psychiatry: Exploring the Work of Suman Fernando in Clinical Practice*. London: Routledge.
Moodley, R., Gielen, U.P. and Wu, R., eds. (2013) *Handbook of Counselling and Psychotherapy in an International Context*. Oxon: Routledge.
Obasi, M.E. (2003) *Ebiriba Enuda: The Legendary March to History*. London: Papyrus Graphic Ltd.

Chapter 2

The troubled birth of Nigeria
Being an exile in my own land

Life under colonialism

In this chapter I will discuss the processes that we, as societies, adopted to deal with the loss of our heritage, of our traditional social environments as a consequence of the exiled social living conditions under the colonial regime – the processes of the 'mourning' of our losses.

I will provide an outline of the political structure of our societies, to make clear to the reader how social relationships were dislocated and ruptured.

To begin with, however, I will draw attention to what, according to Ralph Stacey (2007), is the Europeans' views of society as an entity as well as the position of the individual human beings within it.

Stacey referred to what he termed the modernist position: that is the position in which the individual is his society is autonomous within his society – a state of the *autonomous individual*. Stacey pointed out that in the Middle Ages, there was no notion of an individual subject as a 'self', as an autonomous agent within the society such as exists in the modern-day society.

He/she was defined in relation to a cosmic order so that persons come fully to themselves when they are in touch with that cosmic order that is a universal order of things. The individual is not known for himself except in terms of his/her position within such an order. Thus far, this is how our colonised West African societies understand their universe. Therefore individual identity was related to one's position or role within the social hierarchy.

However, while this notion of society remains by and large so in our colonised societies, the scientific ideas and enlightenment have caused changes in the notions of the individuals and their societies during this period. The Enlightenment philosophers, according to Stacey, formulated a modern notion of the self over a roughly 300-year period of the scientific revolution, which culminated in this modern notion of self – the individual. This modern self is understood as a monad cut off from others and which is aware of itself, and defines itself through processes of introspection and reason. To know something then requires the individual to form a hypothesis about the object and test that hypothesis against an objective reality.

It is no longer a process in which the subject is defined in relation to a cosmic order so that persons come most fully to themselves when they are in touch with the cosmic order in union with God. In that process, knowledge takes the form of the exegesis of God's revelation, answers and solutions depend on explanations believed to have come from God. The modern conception of the individual mind is that it is split off from the body; thinking is split off from emotion and individuals are split off from each other and therefore far removed from the face-to-face type of relationship that is still by and large the type of relationship which is characteristic of our largely oral traditional societies, even in the twenty-first century.

Stacey attributes this modernist concept, as it is called, to the German philosopher Immanuel Kant's (1790) work. Since then another German philosopher Hegel (1807) challenged the particular version of modernism presented by Kant. For him modes of consciousness, ways of life, were constituted in social activities. He saw the individual as a cultural being necessarily dependent on others and who only develops a mind and purposes of his own in interaction with others. Hegel saw the nature of society, culture and therefore modes of thought and consciousness as all evolved in conflicting interactions between people. He emphasised greatly the 'social processes of recognition' and argued that a sense of self arose in social processes of mutual recognition. By that process, an individual can only recognise himself or herself as a 'self', in the recognition of those that he or she recognises. From this perspective, Stacy argued that individual change cannot be separated from change in the groups to which the individual belongs nor can change in the group be separated from changes in the individual. This way of thinking takes us away from the modern notion of 'self' as the autonomous individual and takes us to a notion of self as interdependence of people whose individual selves are constituted in their interaction with one another.

I would argue here that in addition to this, a second factor arises from this shift from the modernists' perspectives. It highlights the close relationship between people's social network and their identity as people of particular cultural origins. I would argue further that this way of thinking about human relationships and interactions is akin to the basic foundation of the Object relations theorists, Brown and Pedder (1979). They questioned Freud's early psychoanalytic view of sexuality as a pleasure-seeking drive present from birth as being too centred on the individual and his gratification. This is, of course, given that this was in the context of the child's developmental processes from his/her birth. The Object relations theorists from Fairbairn (1952), Winnicott (1965), Guntrip (1969), to Balint (1975) suggested that the primary motivational drive in man is to seek relationships with others. The search would necessarily be carried out through the means appropriate to the stage of development.

Stacey pointed out that the process sociologist Norbert Elias (1991) acknowledged Hegel's influence in emphasising the essential interdependence of people. Elias (1978) described the evolution of Western civilisation saying that the network of human activities tends to become increasingly complex, far-flung and closely knit. More and more groups, and with them more and more individuals, tend to become dependent on each other for their security and for the satisfaction of their needs in ways which, for the greater part, surpass the comprehension of those involved.

Norbert Elias (1991) also pointed out that the interplay of the actions, purposes and plans of many people, is not itself something intended or planned and is ultimately immune to planning. I would argue that Norbert Elias' statement implies that cultural factors of a people evolve according to their needs and social circumstances. Hence the political structure of the Igbo societies, for example, is unlike those of some of the other societies included in the country of Nigeria, such as the Yoruba kingdom in the South West, the Efiks in the South East as ourselves the Igbos, the Edo kingdom in the Midwest, all within the amalgamation of the country of 'Nigeria'.

We, the Igbos, are governed by a non-centralised system of rule. Hence the political structures of our societies are exemplified by the functions of two distinct social groups within them: the village communities and different compounds representing groups from within the villages. Each village exists as an autonomous entity, managing its affairs as necessities dictate to it but, in the final analysis however, everyone within each compound in the villages is subordinate to the principles of the myth of the power of the 'spirit of the ancestors' from which all members of the village derive their solidarity. Each compound or lineage, as the compounds are also known, consists of kin-based groups of children or descendants from the same father who is at the head of the compound and who is known to all in the Igbo societies, as 'Onyenwezi' (The owner and controller of the compound).

The children are not usually always all from the same mother, as the culture of polygamy that allows a man to marry more than one wife has been a common cultural practice throughout all of our societies. It has remained so even today and in spite of Christianity's attempt to abolish it. It is this cultural practice that has created the situation in which descendants from one man may not all be children of the same mother but would be members of this kin-based group – the Umunnas – (children of the same father) in the compound or lineage.

There is a strong solidarity among the different Umunna groups of the same compound – that is, various groups of children of different fathers of the compound. The solidarity is often so strong that the strict boundary that separates one from the other becomes so blurred that all the members of the different compounds or lineages in a village call themselves 'Umunna', as if they were sons of the same father rather than just descendants of different fathers of the village. Ideally 'Umunnas' are civil, respectful and protective towards one another and one another's interests and welfares.

'Onyenwezi' – literally translated this means the owner of the Ezi, the compound – has the overall responsibility and control of the compound Ezi.

Usually the Ezi would be named after him and the descendants from that Ezi are identified by the name of the controller. As an example the author is identifiable as of the Ndi Okerezi compound and subsequently my descendants hold the moral and ritual rites and obligations of the compound. He performs sacrificial rites as necessary to appease God and the 'gods' and to ensure the welfare of all the inhabitants of the compound. He is responsible for settling disputes between people and for performing such social functions as naming ceremonies of newborn babies of the compound or alternatively for delegating somebody to carry out such duties. The eldest male son of Onyenwezi, is known as his Okpara – his firstborn – and he is at the head of the Umunna group or lineage by virtue of being the firstborn of his father's male children. He ranks above all other children of his father. (The word Okpara is the generic name for all firstborn male children of any Igbo.) He is regarded as the most important one of the children and he has the duty to and obligation of acting as the intermediary between members of his lineage and the ancestors. The Okpara lineage head is in charge of the totem symbol of authority known as the 'Ofo' as well as being in charge of the 'Ofo' totem symbol of priesthood. Priests in charge of shrines and the 'dibias' – the medicine men and women – also hold 'Ofo' totem symbol but only as a ritual symbol of priesthood.

The responsibility of performing sacrificial rites on behalf of all members of the compound to the earth deity – 'ali' – also rests with the Okpara. It is the requirement according to custom that the Okpara is informed about all planned political actions because he is expected to give the final guide where there is concern that the action to be undertaken may conflict with customs and traditions.

Other than that, he must not interfere with the internal affairs of the lineage. Okpara has the power to punish all those who misbehave within his domain by virtue of his authority as the holder of the 'Ofo' totem symbol. However, in practice he usually only warns and threatens to punish so that the offence could be pardoned, and such threats are usually enough being regarded as amounting to loss of face in the community for the errant individual or group of people as the case may be. To be in a position of being threatened with a curse by such an important person who also happens to be the intermediary between every member of the community and the spirit of the ancestors is not an enviable one. People would therefore work towards reconciliation rather than towards acrimony for the sake of peace and security of the community as a whole. People feel morally obliged to act within the norms to maintain peace and security.

All these political structures were in effect dismantled by the colonial ruling policies and existed only in theory and kept alive largely in the memories of those who had lived with them and by them before the colonialists arrived in our societies to rupture and to dislocate them. Nor were there alternative mechanisms provided for our ruling ourselves or for maintaining social order and security. Our rulers, whose duty was by virtue of the authority vested in them according to our traditions, remained rulers also but mainly in theory, having been stripped of their authorities by the colonial policies. In doing so, the colonialists also stripped us of our cultural traditions and dignity, showing another evidence of the dislocation and rupture of the structures of our political institutions and heritage.

I argue strongly that the consequences of colonialism in our West African societies had detrimental consequences on us, the natives. For example, the issue that I discussed in Chapter One that has had a profound effect on me, the author. They have had long-lasting and lingering effects on most of the population as is evident in the group sessions discussed in Chapter Five where many of the participants were able to recall and narrate memories of their experiences under the British colonial rule. The prominent citizens of our societies at different levels of professional and social standing who experienced life under the colonial tutelage carry some mental scars from that experience.

All this raises the question of what we could in fact do to deal with our wounded pride and dignity as human beings who feel that they had been so grievously wronged by the White man's interference with our lives.

Garza Guerrero (1974) in his theory of culture shock postulated that the fundamental element of defence against such culture shock takes the form of a process of mourning the loss, such as our freedom to our heritage and including the fantasy of more losses.

This was a matter that we had to deal with by ourselves as we could not hope to engage the British colonialists in an act of war or any form of hostilities to gain some satisfaction. The discussion groups that were one of the means of collecting data on our people's experiences were of course formal groups. But they indicated how most people had instinctively been dealing with their emotional scars even during the period that the colonialists were still occupying our societies as our direct rulers because we were virtually in states of culture shock from which we of necessity had to recover.

In the context of people deprived of and alienated from our traditional cultural heritage, we mourned for our cherished communal lifestyle shared by all of a common heritage. Our mourning process for this loss followed certain phases during which we began to realise how we were gradually and increasingly losing our identity to imitations of the White man's cultural values. We began to panic because of the fear of becoming uncertain of our integrity and authority. We became preoccupied with thoughts of the precious things that we were being deprived of, what we were fond of, our treasured past, and good object relations, which we had when we were free and in full control of our life activities.

It is this threat of losing our identity that also prompted us to identify with some of the alien cultural values as part of the process of *adapting* to some conditions to enable us to survive under the unavoidable exilic social conditions to which we were consigned. This mechanism of adaptation also represented one of our defence strategies against our oppressions and the traumas of the culture shock and building some hope of recovering some of the good objects that we had lost because of the dislocation and rupturing of our traditional cultural traditions by the British colonial ruling policies.

I was not yet born when Britain colonised us and my early life was spent farther away from the capital cities and the main administrative headquarters of the colonialists. The alien British cultures were slower to arrive at these more remote regions of our societies. So too did the degree of these effects of the British colonial regime on our cultural practices vary from region to region. Even from town to town in our societies, the colonial controls were often slow to arrive. The by-laws of the colonial rulers also varied from region to region; consequently, a number of our traditional cultural practices survived longer in some places than in others.

People living in these farflung areas were categorised as British-protected people, whereas those living in the capital cities such as Lagos were categorised as British subjects. All of our societies were nevertheless British colonies. This affected the degree of need to adapt to the colonialists' cultures and the degree to which the native traditional cultures were ruptured and dislocated in the different areas.

As our process of mourning our losses and separations entered a second phase, as it were, we were encouraged through the strength of our egos to adapt to and identify with those British cultural values that least contradicted our own and which also attracted the least scrutiny from the watchful eyes of the colonial policy makers.

Restriction from areas of hallowed ground, such as where a tree with spiritual powers was standing, necessitated adopting some other tree which had not been known to be imbued with the spiritual power.

It was not unusual for people to say, 'Oh but it is the way that 'Beke' – the White man – does it', and with that they would grin and bear an otherwise unacceptable situation. This made it easier to adapt even though in some cases the adaptation proved to be merely a poor imitation of the British culture. Such a situation often drew the response of the British colonialists to the effect that our poor imitations or poor efforts to follow their examples were evidence of the degree of our primitiveness that we could not do even the simplest of things well.

In all this there is another factor to be considered, which I believe affected how far we were or were not competent enough to imitate the British: that is how far we were prepared to go along with acquainting ourselves with the British ways of doing things despite the strangeness of these alien cultural practices to us.

This represented another form of adaptive behaviour similar to that demonstrated by the reactions of the Black Victorians or the Black British to the effects of the British education system imposed on us. They identified with the British Victorian values much more exhaustively, condemning and disassociating themselves from our traditional ways of life. Whether the Black Victorians were handicapped by a type of social upbringing in which they were not privileged to deeply engage in entrenched traditional culture and were therefore devoid of patriotic spirit and with weak ego is a matter of conjecture. Or perhaps the method or degree of coercions to which they were exposed was done with greater efforts and enthusiasm than it was for the other people of our societies who had different attitudes to the colonial cultures.

That also, I would say, is a matter of conjecture that nevertheless represented an example of the members of our societies who did not resist very much against the oppressive British regime.

Irrespective of which of these factors was at play, the behaviour of the Black Victorians demonstrated a pragmatic survival technique of flight in the face of perceived danger when the true patriots stood firm to fight against what they perceived as alien and a danger to their culture and ways of life. They even shared some of the British views on our cultural traditions as being inferior and primitive when compared with those of the British.

Following the efforts to adapt to some of the British ways of life and subject to the relevant conditions, we endeavoured to ensure that we could adjust to those British values that we had acquired as necessary for our survival. In other words, we aspired to consolidate our newly acquired cultural values or new ways of living.

This often involved experiencing situations which exposed the cultural differences between us and the British and invoked the British colonialists' remarks that we were too primitive to perform even simplest tasks, while we counter remarked that the White people lived too complicated lives with little time to relax.

This perhaps suggests that our two cultures' concepts of time are different from one another.

Again the extent to which we were able or not able to manage our life with the newly acquired British ways depended on how we were emotionally equipped and the importance of what we were endeavouring to acquire for our survival.

In other words, the new object relations formed by adopting some of the colonialists' cultures are organised into some form of *ego identity*. Again some of us seemed more at ease in doing this than others were, and the Black Victorians seemed to be more at ease with this situation than the rest of the society even though in the final analysis they remained at the fringe of things when compared with the British whose culture they were trying to imitate.

In the final analysis, that was as far as they could go: idealising the colonialists' cultural values by identifying with them, that is, the oppressors, for their power.

The last phase of this process of adapting for survival of the loss of free access to the objects of our cultural heritage was the process of integrating these mechanisms to be accepted as part of the super ego ideal and part of the autonomous ego functions; in our traditional contexts, to be integrated as part of our routine daily social actions. This means that it becomes part of the repertoire of actions available to us in our daily life activities.

Sigmund Freud (1917) similarly understands the processes of adjusting to the new and strange circumstances of the exile or émigré's life as being that his libido attaches itself to objects in the new country. In other words, as in our situation, we turned our emotional cravings and urges to those in the new environment we believe can assist us to recreate what we had lost.

According to Freud, our ego withdraws the libido that was formally attached to familiar good objects of our cultural heritage and takes this with it to reinvest in the object that it had selected and adopted in the new environment from which it is seeking its new identity. It is as if the ego cries 'sour grapes' suggesting that those good objects of the previous conditions no longer served their purposes and therefore should be forgotten as soon as appropriate replacements could be found for them from the categories in the new situation or circumstances.

I would argue that both Guerro's and Freud's findings highlight the significance of people's culture to their survival and mental development. That is to have a root to belong to and identify with is vitally essential to the formation of their identity.

In his later assessment of this process of withdrawing the libido from the lost object into itself, as a way of mourning, Freud (1923) reached a revised conclusion that it was in fact a normal process for the ego to develop by looking to replace important good objects that were lost as a result of changes to social conditions.

As I stated earlier here, seen in the context of analytic interpretation of the behaviours of the Black Victorians or the Black English Men so called, for example, I would argue that what I choose to refer to as their cavalier reactions in response to their experience of the impact of the colonialists' dehumanising ruling style towards us amount to taking 'flight' away from their deep emotional pain – a denial.

It was in my view, their way of dealing with their total incapacity and inability to cope with the stresses and strains required to stand up and fight against the British colonial oppressions that were just as alienating, subjugating and humiliating to them as they were to the other members of our societies who made their oppositions to these detrimental excesses of the colonialists' ruling policies known in manners that reflected their true spirit of nationalism.

So then, the Black Victorians chose to deal with ill treatment by our colonisers by acquiescing with their ideologies of valuing and treating us, members of human societies, as less than human. They also chose to promote openly and in contempt of our own traditions, the colonialists' values as being preferable ways of doing things to our native traditional ways. This is even against the background of differences in the cultures of our two peoples.

This gave rise to the development of a culture which is characterised by uncritical acceptance of everything European as being superior to our West African equivalents. This is known as 'Couriferism', and it is a word coined from 'Mr. Courifer', the name of a character in a short story by Adelaide Casely-Hayford (1960).

The sad thing about Couriferism is that it has become endemic in our part of West Africa since it was bequeathed to us by colonial policies through indoctrinations, coercions and other forms of psychic colonisations which were also visited on us by the colonialists. For example, many parents in our societies today strongly believe that the way forward for their children's future lies in their ability to speak and write the English language. There is nothing whatsoever wrong with learning and speaking a foreign language. In fact I would argue that learning and speaking foreign languages places people in an advantageous position in dealing with the world beyond one's own. That can only be to the advantage of any up and coming youngster or any aspiring person. However, what I feel is sad about this preoccupation with learning the English language is that it is meant to be done at the expense of our own native languages. The preoccupation with learning the English language has come at the price of relegating our own native languages to the inferior classes of culture as compared with the value that has been placed on the foreign culture of the English language.

However, unlike the Black Victorians and in contrast to their responses but affected by the same dislocations and ruptures of our traditional cultures, another group in our societies stood up to fight for their right to speak for and defend the authenticity of our cultural traditions. In spite of all the potential risks of stresses and strains that this involved, they insisted that our traditional cultural heritage did not need to be apologised for.

They stood up for our right to observe and practice our cultural traditions, our way of life and for these to be portrayed with loyalty and conformity in order to validate their autochthonous values. This reaction to our exilic conditions of life demonstrated by this group of the members of our societies was clearly in contrast with those of the Black Victorians who chose to acquiesce to the alien cultural values and to debase our own as inferior.

The amalgamation of our otherwise independent and autonomous societies into what came to be named the country of Nigeria and the administration policies that followed meant that members of each of our different societies were spread into the various and different societies that were included and pronounced by the decree of 1914 as the so called one united country of Nigeria. As units of people from different societies could not and cannot speak one another's languages, it was thought to be prudent to teach and encourage everyone to learn to be literate in a common language, the English language. It was therefore made to become our lingua franca and that decision condemned our different native languages to near oblivion.

Many people's occupations were determined by the colonisers and, by virtue of that fact, their economic livelihoods were controlled by the colonisers who determined the economic migratory movements of such people. I shall say more about this fact in Chapter Three when I discuss the type of education policy that our colonisers adopted for us. Furthermore, because our traditional culture is an oral one rather than a literate one, and our natural means of communication among ourselves in each of our different societies is by face-to-face interactions, we had no strong impetus or eagerness to learn literacy even in our own respective languages. We were particularly not keen to be literate in a foreign language of people who had been oppressing us and whose basic instinct toward us as a people was predominantly racially prejudicial.

This hesitancy to embrace education in the foreign language of our colonisers may also be because as Frantz Fanon (1967) observed, 'To speak means above all to assume a culture, to support the weight of a civilisation'. Being colonised by a language has larger implications for one's consciousness. Speaking a foreign language means that one largely accepts or is coerced into accepting the collective consciousness of the foreign culture whose language is spoken. This is especially so regarding the language of the British – the English language – because the British at least at the early times of colonialism identified our black skin features with features of sub-human beings. At the very least our instinct of self-preservation prevented us from colluding with such people who were so racially prejudiced against us and I believe many of whom are deep down still prejudiced against the black-skinned person.

The factor of language as I have discussed it here is only an example of how the reactions of a particular group of the members of our societies to the dehumanising and subjugating attitudes of our colonisers led to a culture of uncritical acceptance of European values as being superior to our native cultural values. Our developed general attitude of preferring to educate our children in the English language in preference to our native languages is used here as an example to illustrate this attitude.

I shall elaborate more on language as one of the important aspects of a peoples' cultural identity in Chapter Three.

I propose then that the reactions of the two groups of the members of our societies – the Black Victorians and those who opposed their mental attitudes to the colonialists – to the effects of the colonial policies, highlights the split in the opinions held by our citizens in different aspects of our lives. This view was also confirmed by the outcome of the interviews and discussions I had with fellow Igbos which is reported in Chapter Five.

Whether this was a fortuitous circumstance as it might appear, or not, is in the final analysis academic. What is clear is the fact that it meant in effect that we were polarised into different camps, one of which gave credence to the colonialists' policies, albeit a small fraction of all the members of our societies, while the other experienced it as repressive and destructive and therefore opposed it.

Yet neither of the two positions was able to rescue us from the psychic injuries that have been caused by the way that the British colonisers treated us, the effects of which, I would argue, continue even today as we roll along in an illusion of being an independent federal country.

The behaviours of the Black Victorians remained as a camouflage over their inner conflict created by the conflicting values of their communal primordial cultural heritages and the alien British cultures with which the colonialists endeavoured to replace ours in order to accommodate their own agenda.

This chapter concludes, then, that, as Igbos, we remain in many ways largely confused within ourselves both as individuals and as societies about who we are. It argues that there are unanswered questions in our minds as societies, raised by our experiences of the colonial rule. What would we have become if the root of our culture and traditions had not been so deliberately attacked, dislocated and ruptured that its central structure could no longer sustain the magnitude of its responsibility? It must be our aspiration then to retrace our roots so as to properly plot our direction to our true future and by that I mean a future which is shaped by the Igbo citizens and seen to be in the best interests of the majority.

I say this fully aware that, in reality, societies are processes and therefore it is difficult to say what is the 'true' future of a society. However, I would argue that it is possible to visualise a future in which the best of one's or society's cultural heritage is appreciated and valued, and in which the citizens feel proud of their natural identity.

I would argue further that a future in which citizens of a society can determine the direction in which they are moving, using their own cultural heritage and are not deterred from freely determining the actions that they take as a people in the process would be as true a future for the society as they can expect. I would argue further that this would be as true for a society as it would be for an individual seeking his true future.

Having presented an outline of the rationale, aims and intentions of this book, and given my personal perspective on the conflicted society into which I was born and grew up, in Chapter Three I will discuss the relationship between our culture and our identity as people in three aspects: our native languages, our traditional system of education and our African Traditional Religions (ATR).

Reference list

Balint, M. (1975) *The Doctor, His Patient and the Illness*. New York: International University Press.
Brown, D. and Pedder, J. (1979) *An Introduction to Psychotherapy*. London: Tavistock Publications.
Casely-Hayford, A. (1960) 'Mista Courifer', in L. Hughes ed., *An African Treasury*. New York: Crown Publishers.
Elias, N. (1978) *What Is Sociology?* Oxford: Blackwell.
Elias, N. (1991) *The Society of Individuals*. Oxford: Blackwell.
Fairbairn, W.R.D. (1952) *An Object-Relations Theory of the Personality*. London: Tavistock Pubs.
Fanon, F. (1967) *Black Skin White Mask*. Translated by C.L. Markmann. New York: Grove Press.
Freud, S. (1917) *Mourning and Melancholis, S.E. XIV*. London: Hogarth Press.
Freud, S. (1923) 'The ego and the id', in *On Metapsychology*. Pelican Freud Library, Vol. 11. Reprint 1991. London: Penguin.

Guerrero, G. (1974) 'Culture shock: Its mourning and the vicissitudes of identity', *Journal of the American Psychoanalytic Association*, 22(2), pp. 408–429.

Guntrip, H. (1969) *Schizoid Phenomena: Object-Relations and the Self*. New York: International University Press.

Hegel, G.W.F. (1807) *The Phenomenology of Spirit*. Translated by A.V. Miller, 1977. Oxford: Oxford University Press.

Kant, I. (1790) *Critique of Judgement*. Translated by W.S. Pluhar, 1987. Indianapolis: Hackett.

Stacey, R. (2007) 'The challenge of human interdependence: Consequences for thinking about the day to day practice of management in organizations', *European Business Review*, 19(4), pp. 292–302.

Winnicott, D.W. (1965) *The Maturational Process and the Facilitating Environment*. New York: International Press.

Chapter 3

Culture, identity and language
Exploring my identity as a group analyst and Igbo man

In the following chapters I intend to explore three aspects of our culture: our native languages and literature; the relationship between our culture and our identity as a people in the context of education; and our African Traditional Religions (ATR). As I have stated earlier on, being raised in two different and conflicting cultures has had a significant impact on my life, on my identity personally and professionally, and obliged me to look back to better understand the roots of the disquiet that I have so often experienced.

The key words here are 'identity' and 'culture'.

The definition of 'identity' in the Webster's Comprehensive dictionary (1991) is:

1 The state of being identical or absolutely the same; selfsameness.
2 Sameness of character or quality.
3 The distinctive character belonging to an individual; personality; individuality.

'Culture' is defined as having seven different meanings. Of all these, it is the sixth definition that I consider as the relevant one for all my references to the word culture in this chapter and in the rest of the book. That is:

> the sum total of the attainment and activities of any specific period, race, or people, including their implements, handicraft, agriculture, economics, music, art, religious beliefs, traditions, language and story.

I aim in this chapter to show that there are relationships between these different aspects of cultural traditions of our colonised societies that I have enumerated above and our identity as a people. I would argue that the colonial ruling policies that interfered with those cultural practices also denigrated our identity as a people and an effect on the characteristics of the culture, hence on their identity: identity according to the third definition that I have given above from the dictionary, is the distinctive character belonging to an individual, his personality and his individuality.

My argument here is that the identity of a society develops according to the culture of the people. That is to say that people's cultural values mould them into the type of identity that they develop and this in turn influences the further development of their culture. It is an interaction that can be enriching, and societies such as that of the UK have voluntarily absorbed many different cultures with their own religions and ways of life over the years. However, the UK has not been colonised for many centuries. Having an alien culture imposed on a society is an entirely different matter, particularly when the colonisers aim to denigrate and destroy the existing culture.

In the following chapters I will discuss the connection between our identity and our culture in the context of three of our important cultural traditions, namely:

1   Our languages and literature
2   Our traditional education system
3   Our religious beliefs

The issue of the relationship between a people's culture and the development of their identity is not a recent one among human civilisations. Many thinkers over time have advanced views on the relationships between people's roots and their identity. According to Jostein Gaarder (1995), as far back as the time of Aristotle (384–322 BC), many thinkers have added their views on the subject of the link between people's identity and their roots.

Foulkes (1964), himself an émigré and the founder of the Institute of Group Analysis London, held the view that man is primarily a social being. Hence Foulkes' concept of group analytic psychotherapy was based on belief in the importance of the relationship between individuals and their social network. The network is not merely of the interpersonal but could be described as transpersonal and supra-personal. Foulkes likened the individuals in their social network to mere nodal points inside the structural entity of their societies, just like neurons in the network of the nervous system. He added that the group or community situation should be the matrix from which to define the position of an isolated individual. With this statement, Foulkes further emphasised his belief that there is a link between an individual's conduct or manner of behaviour and his place of origin.

I would argue that this position represents Foulkes' conviction that there is a strong link between people's identity and their culture of origin. That is, who or what he develops into bears an imprint of his social origin.

As I share Foulkes' assessment of the individual in relation to his society, that he is a nodal point in the social network, I would argue further that the individual is an offspring of his/her social network. That is why in group analysis a person's social nature is viewed as a basic factor of who he or she is, and that how individuals emerge is the result of the type of interactions that they experienced in their community of origin.

Erikson (1968) regarded adolescence as the psycho-social stage of belonging to groups and to finding an identity through belonging to and acquiring identity from those groups. An identity can be both what you are like or what you are different from. The primary impetus is, of course, to belong. Therefore any situation that damages or deprives a people of their root, their natural heritage, has the potential to deny the people of their identity. This is perhaps the unconscious impetus behind the formation of groups of affiliations and establishing sub-cultures with which members of such groups can identify. This again emphasises people's need to belong to a root to which they can associate themselves and can call their own. In it they would feel safe and secure in the knowledge of who they are. If they belong also to a subgroup in their society, they would establish outward signs which would mark them out as members of esoteric groups which share common ideas about life provided that they did not contravene the general rules and norms of the wider society.

Le Roy (1987) also contributed to the view that a relationship exists between people's identity and their roots or place of natural origin, saying that the development of identity, as well as the functioning of the person through it in his actual life, depends on the link between the individual and the collective, both internal and external. In Le Roy's later contribution on the subject (1994), he added that it is the group to which the individual belongs that does the linking.

Even immigrants from a foreign country have to confront the issue of belonging and having a network with which to belong and identify. Until that happens they feel isolated, strange, insecure and unsafe. They seek an environment that is familiar to that which they left behind and from that they would create an environment in which they would belong to and feel safe.

The colonial regime which isolated us from our natural and familiar environment did in effect leave us feeling like exiles in our own societies – because we virtually no longer had a root. Even though we were in our own homelands we had no control over our natural environments. This was my experience and the experience of many other young children of the time. Parents were not sure of the extent of their control over their children. Under such conditions it was no wonder that, as in Le Roy's (1994) terms, individuation was difficult for young people to achieve. Personal identity and psycho-social identity are based on a double transpersonal foundation – the cultural foundation matrix and the family group matrix.

For Erikson, also, the issue of a child's ego development is one which is fraught with crisis for the child; nevertheless it is one from which the child cannot escape. Erikson's view was that there has to be basic trust between the child and the mother/caregiver as the child needs this important factor to be able to progress into the stage of the next crisis in the process of his/her development.

Thus, in addressing the issues of the relationship between the individual's social culture and his/her identity, I share Foulkes' assessment that the individual is a nodal point in the social network and that is why in group analytic practice, the individual's social nature is viewed as a basic factor of who he or she is as a person.

Foulkes' assessment emphasises most emphatically that the individual person cannot be other than a part of a social network, and as such, he exemplifies the attributes and characteristics of his social network, his root, his society.

Evidently, there are many views in agreement with the suggestion that identity formation is clearly a function of people's social network. It is therefore reasonable to argue that an occurrence that affects the structure of the social network will be likely to affect the identity of the people of such a social network, given the concept of interdependence mentioned previously.

The examples of views supporting that statement that I have given above are not intended to suggest that the relationships between our social network and our identity should be taken for granted. Therefore that we can assume that the dislocations and ruptures caused by the colonialists' ruling policies affected our identity as a people.

We were colonised people who were reduced to living as people in exile in their own homeland, and this indeed affected our identity. As a direct result of the colonialists' policies, our citizens were thrown into confusion about their identities when autonomous and independent societies were forced into union with other societies with different social cultures.

The Yoruba people, for example, who comprised various autonomous societies within the geographical areas by the name of Yoruba lands, were deprived of their autonomous power and compelled to change most of their ways of life.

The Igbos, accustomed only to their decentralised system of government, were forced into unintended associations with several of the other independent societies who were otherwise autonomous and independent states themselves.

The Edos kingdom was an independent society, free with their own laws and traditions, free with their own system of kingship and their regulations independent of other nations. However, following the British colonialists' invasion of the Edo kingdom and consequunct disruptions of their culture, looting of their cultural artefacts, symbols of their culture and identity to furnish their own (the British) homeland, the Edo citizens were left bereft of the means of practising their cultural traditions. They were confused about what they had become and in doubt about their identity as a people.

As I pointed out in Chapter Two, another evidence of the relationship between a people's culture and the development of their identity was the emergence of a culture of uncritical acceptance of European cultural values, termed 'Couriferism' – not merely accepting European cultural values without any reservations but establishing that something either material or a pattern of behaviour of European origin is credited with a mark of excellence and approval by our citizens. There are cases in which even the Europeans themselves might feel that their product was substandard, yet the fact that it is a European product served as sufficient credential for our people to accept it as superior to our native alternatives.

Another characteristic of 'Couriferism' is that based on the belief and acceptance that European cultural values were superior to our native cultural values, causing our natives so affected to condemn our own cultural values and to find faults in them to justify their attitude. As an example, millions of foreign currencies are spent importing European secondhand clothing which may be ill fitting, and this is justified by the saying, 'At least you know that it is the right thing'. Yet 'being the right thing' does not always mean that it fits better or that it necessarily enhances the appearance of the wearer. It was not unusual to see people wearing knitted woolen clothes in the hot climate because it looks good on the wearer and most attractive of all because it has 'Made in London' written on the inside of the collar. Yet this happens in societies that were and still are skilled in weaving beautiful fabrics from cotton. These fabrics are now in fashion in Britain and have featured in *Vogue* magazine, for example.

The raw cotton was exported to those European countries who manufacture clothes and exported back to us to spend our foreign currencies on. One reason for our acceptance of this type of business dealing was and remains that we had been coerced into believing that things European were and remain superior to things that are manufactured by ourselves; the 'Couriferism' syndrome.

The bone of contention here is not that Europeans, who are technologically more advanced than our developing societies, are able to manufacture better quality goods. Rather, it is about the mindset that we had been coerced into developing and which sits deep in our psyche. That is, that although we are capable of producing good enough clothes for ourselves, we are distracted from doing so by the belief that we are clearly and simply inferior to the Europeans in all aspects of life. Hence our own manufactured goods are not good enough even for our own use. As a result of this, we discourage our own producers through what amounts to a vote of no confidence in their skill.

In the late nineteenth century, Sir Harry H Johnston (1930) expressed his belief that Europeans alone had, with their white skin, 'evolved beauty of facial features and originality of inventions in thought and deed'. This statement appears prophetic when latterly applied to inventions and productions.

It was never a matter of dispute that Europeans have been well advanced in scientific knowledge beyond the level of our societies, nor was there any attempt to deprive the British of their accustomed ways of life. Except of course to the extent that the two interests militated one against the other, a situation which arose more often than not in the course of our inter-relationships.

In various ways we experienced the material result of the much advanced European technology as impressive and awe inspiring. In varying degrees and in varying circumstances, our citizens became overwhelmed by what confronted them from the Europeans' scientific products. They reacted towards the Europeans as they would to a 'god', by projecting their super ego to the overwhelming force of the European scientific ingenuities. This psychological condition played an important part in creating the mindset that evolved when the White men arrived and marked the beginning of the inter-relationship between us and our colonisers.

Sadly, in the different complexities of our relationships with our colonisers some among us fell victim to what I have referred to as *psychic colonisation*. This phenomenon, as I argued, results from the persistent coercive approach of the colonialists in their ruling policy, and I further argue that it is at the root of the 'Couriferism' syndrome.

This fact was made evident by a culture that developed predominantly among young women who were made to feel so self-conscious of their black skins as being inferior to the white skins of our colonisers that they resorted to washing their skins with chemical compounds. The chemical made their skin lighter but in some cases that was at the risk of developing skin cancer. Yet this culture continued because of the entrenched mentality that white skin was superior to black skin.

Irrespective of the factor of the tropical sun rays tanning skin, the white people convinced these impressionable young women that our darker skin was a sign of our inferiority as a people. Thus these young women saw themselves as inferior beings. This developed into intra-racial rivalries and envy as people within the same social environment competed to acquire lighter skin. Those who succeeded better in lightening their skin claimed that it was a sign that deep down they were superior beings of the race, thus becoming objects of the envy of those who were less successful.

The mindset that developed from the Victorian view of the superiority of white skin over black skin extended to affect people's choice of spouse. People began to equate lighter skin as a mark of beauty, a virtue that should be coveted. The lighter a daughter's skin, the higher price parents asked for a dowry, endorsing the belief that lighter skin added to our female citizens' personae, including in terms of monetary and material values.

The significance of this mindset is that we accepted and engraved in our minds the idea that the European criteria for evaluation and assessment of worth were superior to ours, the natives'.

The depth of this mindset in our consciousness is exemplified by my Vignette 3.1, 'A chance encounter between a school teacher and her ex-pupil in a Nigerian market place'.

Vignette 3.1 A chance encounter between a school teacher and her ex-pupil in a Nigerian market place

A woman once went to one of the large street markets in 'Nigeria' to buy some wares. As she looked round at the goods that were displayed, she saw a display of beautiful pairs of shoes and stopped to admire them

> more closely as the vendor also went closer to promote his goods. The shopper still admiring the shoes with interest asked about their price and at that instance she noticed the vendor as he too noticed the shopper. She thought that he was someone that she had seen before in a different setting and so she asked if that was the case. The vendor replied saying, 'Yes miss, you were my teacher when I was still a student'. The shopper then asked, 'Are you the seller of these beautiful pairs of shoes?'
>
> The vendor replied saying, 'Yes, that is right and I made them too'. The school teacher was full of pride and bought some pairs and went away and showed off her purchase with great pride. Other people shared her pride too, to the extent that they put in orders for some pairs. The teacher went to buy the shoes as ordered and arrived at the stall where her ex-student now shoe maker and vendor was trading.
>
> She saw the shoes beautifully displayed as before but she noticed something else about the shoes. They now had labels on the soles which read 'Made in Italy'. She said to the vendor, 'These shoes look exactly like the ones that you made. Why do you now import these from Italy?' The vendor replied saying, 'I did not import these'. They are the ones that I made. You bought some pairs from me perhaps because you were proud of me because you knew who I was and what I have been able to achieve. Other shoppers who did not know me before know only that I am a Nigerian shoe maker and for that they are convinced that the quality of my shoes are inferior to those made in Italy.
>
> By giving my products an Italian label I changed their identity to those of a higher and superior quality of merchandise in the eyes and minds of our native shoppers. They are now buying more of them than they were doing before'.
>
> At once the European name of Italy, conjured up an automatic aura of superiority over the Nigerian identity.

It illustrates the detrimental effect of some of the reactions that we were coerced into by the type of relationships that the colonialists adopted in their dealings with us. It also gives an indication of the extent to which we were prepared go to protect and maintain the integrity of our occupational skills, demonstrating yet again the effect of our psychology on our perception of the White men thus providing another example of 'Couriferism'.

Sir Harry Johnston's statement about what in my own view amounts to the Victorians' assessment of our potential as a people is illustrated by evidence of the outcome of the colonial policies for our societies, namely concerning education. I argue that because the colonial policies affected our cultures they also affected our identity.

The relationship between our traditional system of education and our identity as a people: the dichotomy between our system and that of our British colonisers

It is important here to reflect on the disruption that the social relationship that was created by the British colonial policies brought to the psychological lives of our developing children. The coercive approach of the colonialists casts doubts in their minds about the authority of our various culture-carriers. For example, the priests of our religious shrines, our traditional rulers who provided our system of education, which includes mechanisms for our children's developmental processes – all these were adversely disrupted.

Rumours about the limitless powers of the colonisers often filtered through to our more remote societies causing anxieties about what new laws they might bring which would prevent us from following our traditional system of bringing up our children. We were always aware of how important it was for us to maintain our ways of life if we were to preserve our cultural traditions for posterity. Therefore, educating our future generations accordingly was important to us. Consequently any actions such as those arising from the British system of education which abolished our own traditions were seen as militating against the survival of our culture, adversely affecting our identity. This seriously challenged our integrity as a people and understandably was a cause of anger and feeling of humiliation.

The experience was felt as one of the most cruel social impositions on our traditional cultural identity. Before the advent of the Western literate system of education, our West African native children were inducted into the traditional way of life by formal teaching in initiation ceremonies and by informal teaching in seeing and following the examples of grown-ups through watching and imitating. As Obiechina (1975) pointed out, children participated in the everyday life of the community and by so doing they came to know the rights and duties of the individual, the values, beliefs and mores of the community. They came to know the sanctions and etiquette of social behaviour.

In the same way they acquired knowledge of the material repertoire of the culture and in this way, cultural content and behaviour were transmitted to the individual by contact and deliberate induction.

The experience of an individual member of this society was limited only to his immediate social-cultural environment. Experience outside this was beyond his apprehension as it was not accessible to him through his traditional education. It was not necessary to move away from our familiar environment to a special enclosure called school. It was not difficult for us to relate to objects and situations because we were already in our familiar environments.

It is not remote in my memory to recall the anxiety and suspicions that were aroused by the requirement each morning, to get up, wash, get dressed and arrive at the schoolhouse for lessons.

On the contrary, it is relatively still fresh in my mind how, as school children, we resented being kept away from hunting birds, setting traps for rabbits and fishing, harvesting wild berries. In the process of acquiring these experiences, we come to know the habitats and the characteristics of the different creatures that we encounter, thereby becoming familiar with our natural environments. Our life becomes organised around these – our – natural environments. In some instances, people identify so closely with the characteristics of some of the features of the environment that they claim, believing it to be true, that they are for instance, the ferocious leopard-Agu or the mighty oak tree-Oji or some other feature of the environment. Accordingly they would adopt the names of these features and become known by the names. Generally speaking, all members of a society identify with their social environment and that is at the root of their identity as people.

It was against the background of this traditional system of education and its consequences that the British system of education was introduced in at least some localities of our native societies.

The introduction of the Western system of education to our societies

Thus, the introduction of Western education broke the psychic insularity that is characteristic of our traditional education system. Our traditional system together with its accompanying values was replaced with British colonial literacy education. With that came the corpus of Western civilisation, its institutions and its values, arts and sciences, its philosophies and its theology as Obiechina explained.

One of the consequences was the creation of Westernised urban settlements distinct from ours. Urbanisation, for those who had successfully achieved it, meant moving away from the community where status and social hierarchy had determined their place in the society and where they counted in terms of their groups of affiliations. In the social structure of my Abiriba community as I stated in Chapter One, a person's social status was and is determined by the social hierarchy of his group of affiliation.

I argue that in assessing these two systems of education, we can see the extent to which, with all the merits that could be attributed to it, the British system of education clearly militated against the survival of many of our traditional cultures.

As Obiechina points out:

> Through the introduction of literacy, the corpus of Western, indeed world civilisation, its institutions and values, arts and sciences, philosophies and theology, its aesthetic values, and the artefacts of its material culture were made available to people in West Africa.

He points out further that James Coleman (1958) said of this that it 'awakened new aspirations, quickened the urge towards new emulation and provided the notions'.

The consequences of the British system of education that was introduced to us

The dangers inherent in the British education system and the colonialists' values were exposed by our West African writers and likewise, many other West African patriots were also able to highlight their concerns. Suffice it to say here that Chinua Achebe, one of the novelists, was endowed with the ability to enter imaginatively into the lives of the traditional characters. He was able to explore the strains to which his characters were exposed as a result of the disruptive effect of the foreign culture on their relatively stable and self-sufficient culture in which they grew up.

I would argue that this encounter between the colonialists' imposed culture through their education system and the great efforts of our West African writers to expose the consequences of their imposition highlights two important factors: one being the existence of two divergent cultures competing for supremacy, one of which, the colonialists' was indeed dominant over ours, the natives'.

The other factor is the awakening of our consciousness by our West African writers to ways that the British education system dislocated and ruptured our native cultural traditions and institutions. It militated against their aims and relegated them to a position of inferiority. It led to the development of mass media which disrupted our old social order and accelerated social changes beyond the rate we could endure. It is my contention that this brought about social disharmony, confusion, disorientation and loss of sense of identity.

Contribution of the West African novelists to maintaining our identity

We have many reasons to be grateful for the contributions of our West African novelists, such as Chinua Achebe, Emmanuel Obiechina, Cyprian Ekwensi, Amos Tutuola, R.E. Obeng, Wole Soyinka and others, as without their consciousness of our social predicament we would have all but lost our birth rights to the colonialists' zeal for their economic exploitation. They turned the tide of the seeming apathy as a measure of their alertness to the danger that threatened us in all aspects of our life. Their conscious awareness of the prevailing social climate induced by the oppressive regime of British imperialism awakened the literate population and drew attention to the dislocation and rupturing of our national culture. This evoked a spirit of cultural nationalism.

By way of illustrating the impact of Western civilisation on our native Igbo traditional cultures, Chinua Achebe used the example of two essentially traditional characters, Okonkwo, in the novel *Things Fall Apart* (1958), and Ezuela, in *The Arrow of God* (1964), and how they had been affected. In the third, *No Longer at Ease* (1960), he illustrated the disintegrative forces of modernism on tradition through the character of a Western-educated native of our society. These stories reveal a series of events in which the colonists gradually infiltrated, introducing their religious beliefs and ways of organising communities. With the following extract from *Things Fall Apart*, Achebe illustrated the gradual spread of their ideas in our communities:

> When they had all gathered, the white man began to speak to them. He spoke through an interpreter who was an Igbo man, though his dialect was different and harsh to the ears of Mbanta . . . but he was a man of commanding presence and the clansmen listened to him. He said he was one of them, as they could see from his colour and his language. The other four black men were also their brothers, although one of them did not speak Igbo. The white man was also their brother because they were all sons of God. And he told them about this new God, the Creator of all the world and all the men and women. He told them that they worshipped false gods, gods of wood and stone . . . he told them that the true God lived on high and that all men when they died went before Him for judgement. Evil men and all the heathen who in their blindness bowed to wood and stone were thrown into a fire that burned like palm-oil. But good men who worshipped the true god lived for ever in this happy kingdom. 'We have been sent by this great God to ask you to leave your wicked ways and false gods and turn to Him so that you may be saved when you die,' he said.
>
> (Achebe, 1958: 104)

He thus highlighted the consequences of colonial imperialism in these three novels and alerted readers to its dangers. Some of the literate citizens who had contacts with the villages took their newfound experiences to them through the common characteristic of oral traditional culture, that is, through the use of narrative communication. Achebe was very successful in reaching the people and his success lay in his ability to imagine accurately how the lives of his traditional characters worked. Even with his middle-class education and upper middle-class high profile job, he had the ability to enter imaginatively into the lives of his characters. Even though he had never experienced the actual circumstances of his characters, such as Okonkwo or Ezuela, it was to his immense credit that he was able to portray them and their circumstances convincingly. In this way he demonstrated his capability for imagining people's thinking in their circumstances and in their historical setting.

In Obiechina's view, which I share, Achebe has done more than any other West African novelist in recreating the classic traditional village setting as he demonstrated in his novels, *Things Fall Apart* and *The Arrow of God*. His gift for atmospheric immediacy is illustrated in the first few lines of *Things Fall Apart*, in which he established the social and physical settings of the novel and its intellectual outlook, based around the character Okonkwo and his social standing in the village. Another notable factor in evaluating the contributions of the West African writers to our awareness of the detrimental effects of colonial policies was the ability of the writers to convey their messages accurately to their readers — especially given that most were educated in the British system of education and wrote in the English language — which, as such, could be said to be British culturally bound. It is reasonable to assume that it required more skill than being able to read and write English to be able to convey certain ideas to people of a predominately oral traditional culture than it would be to those who had the literacy cultural background of English people.

For our West African writers, especially Achebe, it was their familiarity with the use of proverbs that enhanced their ability to convey the true circumstances of our traditional cultural life in our coexistence with our colonisers. As I state in Chapter Four, proverbs perform an ideological function in that they make available the ideas and values that are encapsulated in the memorable easily accessible 'seeds' or kernels. In other words, they are a collection of detailed observations of an entire system of thoughts and feelings which represent the collective view of the society. Equipped with their knowledge of the use of proverbs, the novelists' and writers' contributions to our awareness of the detrimental effects of colonial policies have great value and merit great appreciation.

Obiechina (1975) draws attention also to the work of Wole Soyinka (1965), particularly in his novel *The Interpreter*, in which he demonstrated his tendency towards historical and cultural continuity. Generally he derives his conception of life as a continuum from the African traditional worldview and specifically from his Yoruba metaphysics. Another novelist, Ayi Kwei Armah, through a tradition of parabolic narrative and well-chosen illustrative images, dealt with the theme of central social corruption in our West African societies. William Conton (1960) in *The African* used the setting of the issues that confront Africans today to compare the way that he sees himself as an African, using his feelings about nationalism, pan-Africanism, apartheid, to express such themes in his novels.

Each novelist displays wide knowledge of particular social conditions and proceeds to alert us to the threats that confront us as a people because of the colonial ruling policies that imprison us in our own societies. This state, which I have also compared to being in a state of exile in one's own native society, is felt much more when one compares it with the quite different lifestyles in the Western metropolis of the colonisers. The readers in our societies were thus given an opportunity and privilege of knowing about these different situations. Indeed, the West African novelists adopted various styles and approaches to their novels and this added value to their contributions in keeping alive in our consciousness our cultural heritage against the flowing tide of colonial antagonism.

As Obiechina observes, Achebe (1964b) himself stressed that the writer's duty was to infuse the present generations of Africans with a sense of pride in their traditional life and culture. Cyprian Ekwensi (1963), another novelist, indicated his aim as a writer when he defined African writing as 'writing which reveals the psychology of the African'.

Achebe's character of cultural nationalism, which extended beyond his writing skill to his acute observation skill, enabled him to see the bias of the non-West African writers who wrote about our societies and which, as Achebe saw it, was a result of their dogmatic mindset on their ruling system.

In his latest book, *Home and Exile*, Achebe observed how colonial writers categorised the Igbo people as a 'tribe', a group of (especially primitive) families or communities, linked by social, religious or blood ties and usually having a common culture and dialects, and a recognised leader. The Igbo people do not fit this definition of a tribe. Furthermore, Achebe pointed out that, being an Igbo man, he could not have been invited to deliver the 1998 McMillan-Stewart lecture to a Harvard University audience, no less, if the Igbos were primitive people! A further point that Achebe made on the definition of Igbos as a 'tribe' was that although Igbo people speak one language which has many major and minor dialects, they do not speak one dialect as is characteristic of a tribe according to most definitions. Finally, Igbo people regard not having one recognised leader as the defining principle of their social and political identity. In other words we, the Igbos, see that as being what being Igbo is about – because we have a segmentary type of political rule and are not governed by one monarch.

For all the above, we fit more into the category of a nation, far removed from the category of a tribe. Here again is an illustration of how a West African novelist devoted his skill and energy to defending our culture from attacks by the colonialists. At the same time, he made available to the wider population of our people knowledge of how we were at risk of being completely robbed of our cultural traditions and institutions.

There are many examples of great efforts by our West African writers to bring to our consciousness the nature of our relationships with our colonisers. Unlike the French West Africans, our writers did not glamorise their African heritage and did not feel their heritage needed defending. They did not feel that they needed to apologise for our cultural heritage, simply wanting our traditional life and culture to be portrayed with strict conformity to the truth. Obiechina had pointed out that it was for this reason that 19th century scholars like Blyden and Horton had campaigned for a West African university where African culture would be studied and therefore restored to dignity. In so doing, the influence of the European colonisers, with its crushing effect on the minds of the Black West Africans, could be checked.

The spread of the new cultural influence, however, resulted in an increased number of people who were able to read the English language and vernacular newspapers, watch events of other foreign cultural values transmitted through television and also listen to radio broadcasts. These are all the outcome of British education and they were in contrast with the culture that previously prevailed among many of our people who listened to fables, participated in folklore, practised dance rhythms and drumming, and listened to various forthcoming events as they were declared by the town crier. The usual culture of face-to-face interaction and trust in one another, which was typical of our oral traditional culture, was seriously threatened as the British jurisprudence was applied to us in its place and trust among people no longer had value.

In this way yet again, the colonialists' system of education militated against our own values. Because of our entrenched cultural traditions, we could not fully adopt and internalise their values because they were forced on us and were not meant for people of our societies – our geographical climates, our geology, ethnography, family and kinship structure.

The relationship between our African Traditional Religions, one of the most important aspects of our cultural traditions, and our identity as a people

The significance of my giving this account of our African traditional religious beliefs, which are sustained through our traditional system of education, is to show that in their eagerness to introduce their religious belief, the colonialists introduced a system of education that was calculated to be detrimental to ours.

The British colonisers of West Africa in the 19th century brought with them their own religious cultural traditions. Missionaries were the first to visit Nigeria in the late nineteen and early twentieth centuries. These early visitors were instrumental in setting the scene that met the colonialists when they started to arrive to our coasts. They served the colonial powers as an *avant garde* to expand into the new regions of our societies and they were the first white men to be seen by our native citizens (Achebe, 1958).

Their initial task was to bring about the abolition of the slave trade so as to divert commercial interest away from their human product to the Africans' vast natural resources. In this way, trading between our West African societies and Europe would, it was expected, be on a healthier and more mutually beneficial basis. There were those among the British, such as Sir Thomas Fowell Buxton, who saw this first encounter between the Europeans and our nation as necessary for the reason of saving Africa from the evils of the slave trade. Crowder (1962), however, would argue that the commercial interest was of paramount importance, more so than religious concerns.

There was outcry in England against the horrors of the slave trade, backed up by the first-hand accounts of native Africans such as Olaudah Equiano in the late eighteenth century, who described vividly the mistreatments of the slaves.

There was nevertheless the issue of the impending first encounter between the missionaries and the strange cultures of the African Traditional Religions

(ATR). Our high tribal cultural diversity made it difficult for the missionaries to know what to expect when they ventured into in the different areas of our societies. They had come to change our lives which is what conversion effectively amounted to. If successful, this meant erasing our pre-colonial societies, including our religions.

The missionaries' plans were made on assumptions of European supremacy over us and therefore overlooked our cultural richness. That same assumption was taken as a legitimate reason for being in our part of the world with such impunity as was the case. Yet they often found us repulsive both in appearance and in behaviour.

What then were the characteristics of our traditional religions which the colonial missionaries had come so far to coerce us to turn away from? If there are elements in our traditional religions that have potential to prevent rather than support democratic cultures in our West African societies, what may these be, and what made the missionaries so eager to come to convert us from our religious beliefs?

We held in reverence our sacred places, people and objects. For us there is no dichotomy between the secular and the religious; our whole life is enfolded by religion. Any distinctions between the visible and the invisible are treated as merely artificial, therefore there is no conception of a completely secular world.

A person's enduring happiness is not deemed as concentrated on the person's afterlife; life itself is cyclic, going from birth to death and to rebirth. Therefore, concentration is on the totality of the person's well-being in his life and afterlife. Man is not just *homo religious* in the classical sense for the Africans; he does practically everything religiously.

There are other issues which divide Christianity from ATR. These concern the matter of African traditions in totality, which is at the heart of being an African. For instance, in the matters of the veneration of our ancestors and the spirit world, what are the cultural aspects of these vitally important factors of our life as a people that we need to consider from the theological, sacramental, liturgical and canonical points of view regarding them? The question arises also of the place of our cultural practices in the event of our conversion to Christianity, given its tenets for the theological, sacramental, liturgical and canonical doctrines. How far can African Christian converts go in venerating ancestors? What should be the attitude of Christians about the traditional practice of libation in honour of the ancestors, and should the ancestors themselves be expressly mentioned in some liturgical or para-liturgical Christian celebrations?

The missionaries certainly did not accept our brand of piety and were determined to disrupt and dislocate our practices from their roots without consideration for their value to us: the people, for whom these were the pivot of their daily lives. Another issue concerns Greco-Roman influences on Christianity, which conflicted with the ATR by emphasising the division between body and soul, whereas in African categories of thought, as in the Jewish ways of thinking, the human being is considered in his or her wholeness and life is seen in its totality and not parts. For the ATR in their true forms to put aside the concept that divides the human person into body and soul, and choose a theology of wholeness, is to put aside the Christian theology of body and soul separated one from the other.

The basis of ATR are thus, religious tolerance, pluralism and, unlike Islam and Christianity, they are local and are adhered to by specific kinship-based societies. According to the eminent theologian John Mbiti (1969), each African people had its own religion with different gods, cosmogonies, myths of origin, specific rituals and the sacred. The ATR often take the name of the people who follow and worship according to the tenets as, for example, the Yoruba religion is spoken of as the religion of the Yoruba people.

In the same way we, the people of the Igbo nation, have our Iyi Eruru, Otisi Biyom and many others. These have their background and origin in the common ancestries of each of our respective cultural social group with its common set of myths, gods, secret societies, and religious practices. In societies in which our ATR prevailed, boundaries between temporal and secular authority were blurred, so authorities were in the hands of the chiefs who then had the authority to officiate over the matters of the religious rites. Sacrificial rites to appease the gods and spirits of the ancestors are the responsibilities of such heads of the societies.

ATR are highly syncretic and tolerant of a wide range of other religions beliefs. They provide local communities with a high degree of political and religious autonomy (Diagne, 1967), hence the Ghanaian Rulers were content to convert to Islam and establishing that as the official court religion while at the same time insisting upon continuing to fulfil their religious obligations under the old religion (Levtzion, 1973).

The Mandinka rulers of the Mali Empire also show this characteristic of the ATR when after they adopted Islam; they permitted the vassa states and local communities within the empire to practice their own religions without any coercion. These show a high degree of pluralistic characteristics, yet they were the ones that the colonial missionaries came to change into Christianity.

Attitudes of the colonial missionaries to our African Traditional Religions and the processes of conversions

As long as the Christian Churches were satisfied that our ATR customs and rites did not conflict with the 'divine laws' of their Church, they were prepared to accept them. Thus, we were allowed to follow faith traditions as it suited the colonialists, preserving some elements but forbidding others.

In Pope Pius X1's address to the directors of the Pontifical Mission Works, he stated that the specific character, the traditions, the customs of each nation, must be preserved intact, so long as they are not in contradiction with the divine law. He went on to say that the missionary was an apostle of Christ, and his task was not to propagate European civilisation in mission lands. However, it was to train and guide other people, some of whom glory in their ancient and refined civilisation, as to prepare and dispose them for the willing and hearty acceptance of the principles of Christian life and behaviour. These other people were obviously the African natives. That meant that when it came to the attitude towards other religion and religious practices of people such as non-Christians and non-Jews, these were considered as those of pagans whose gods were idols, silver and gold, the work of human hands. They were regarded as having mouths that did not speak, eyes that did not see, and ears that did not hear and there was no breath in their mouth.

According to Chidi Denis Isizoh writing under the title 'Dialogue with African Traditional Religion in Sub-Sahara Africa: The Changing Attitude of The Catholic Church', this is the picture that was painted of the African traditional religions by those at the head of the Christian Missionaries. A rather uncomplimentary image, I would argue.

On the basis of that impression of the ATR, the Christian missionaries assumed the role of delivering the souls of the Africans from eternal damnation as it were, as a matter of religious duty.

Chidi Denis Isizoh pointed out also that:

> in *Rerum Ecclesiae*, Pope Pius X1 considered it a great act of charity on the part of missionaries to withdraw 'pagans . . . from the darkness of superstition' in order to instruct them 'in the true faith of Christ'. Thus each missionary, as ambassador of Christ, must 'bravely face all hardships and difficulties, as long as he could snatch a soul from the mouth of hell'.

The Pontiff also encouraged vocation to the Priesthood especially for 'the heathens particularly those who are still savages and barbarians'. He urged European missionaries to have patience, saying:

> if you find extreme slowness of mind in the case of men who live in the very heart of barbarous regions, this is due to the conditions of their lives, for, since the exigencies of their lives are limited, they are not compelled to make great use of their intelligence.

This desire to save us from damnation, superstition and darkness by instructing us in the true faith of Christ, extended beyond merely giving us the instructions. They decided to include overall cultural advancement and civilisation for us, the uncivilised peoples.

Towards achieving that end, they introduced the European system of education that I discussed earlier in this chapter. At the same time they preached a theology of discontinuity, which urged Africans to break with the ATR and embrace Christianity.

For us, the people of the Igbo nations in particular, and the Efiks and The Ibibio people, these early missionaries inserted in the missionary catechism of the Christian faith, a list of what they considered to be mortal sins and therefore what we should avoid doing so as not to be guided to profanity.

Yet as a matter of fact, most of these were what according to the means of practising our traditional religions we needed to do against the background of our high sense of the sacred.

Changing attitudes toward the African Traditional Religions by the Christian religious groups

There have been gradual but determined moves within Christian religious groups to re-examine their attitudes towards African traditional religions.[1] This is so, particularly as there is also growing awareness of their function in the lives of the people whom they serve. It was in conjunction with this aim that the African Synod encouraged Episcopal Conferences in Africa in cooperation with universities and Catholic institutes, to set up study commissions especially for matters concerning the veneration of ancestors and the spirit world.

The Catholic position is to reject nothing of what is true and holy in different religions. The Council urged all Christians to enter with prudence and charity into discussion and collaboration with members of other religions. While witnessing to their own faith and way of life, they should acknowledge, preserve and encourage the spiritual and moral truths found among non-Christians, also their social life and culture.

Although specific reference was made in *Nostra Aetate* to relations with Muslims and Jews, ATR was not mentioned by name, not until after three years in 1969, almost a decade after the colonialists had ceased their occupations. Then Pope Paul V1, the first to visit sub-Sahara Africa, spoke gloriously about Africa's rich traditions, culture and religion. In his first encyclical letter, *Ecclesiam Suam*, the Pontif mentioned by name 'followers of the great religions of Africa and Asia' and went on to extol the various precious elements found in the African worldview that the Church appreciates and respects. Then there was an acknowledgement of the need to give attentive consideration to the moral and religious values of the ancient African religious cultures. It was acknowledged that the most important element generally found in the spiritual concept was the idea of God as the first ultimate or ultimate cause of all things and the presence of God permeates African life as the presence of a higher being, personal and mysterious.

In conclusion however, in spite of the obstacles imposed by various colonial administrative policies, there has been evident softening of attitudes towards ATR. Much of this is due to the excellent work done by scholars in African Studies who are becoming even more articulate in their presentation of both Christianity and ATR, according to Cardinal Thiandoum, the important place that they occupy in the moulding of the African personality is appreciated.

Religion is part of the curricula of our traditional education; in fact it is one of the most important. It was also part of the curricular in the British system of education that they adopted for us. However, whilst on the one hand the colonial Christian missionaries were strenuously promoting the virtues of the Christian religion, they were on the other hand equally strenuously denigrating the religions of the host societies. Our traditional religions were condemned and branded as fetishism and paganism.

My generation experienced this British colonial prejudicial attitude towards our cultural practices in the celebration of occasions of birth, death, religious rites and other ritual events. These occasions were opportunities for receiving traditional education through the adults and older members of the societies doing and being observed, being watched and being imitated by the younger members. These practices were however branded and treated as primitive practices of a primitive culture.

As such we, with our traditions, were then treated as mere distractions from the colonisers' main objectives of exploitation of our human and natural resources. Therefore this part of our education was not only ignored but was discouraged.

One of the ways of enhancing this impression that they formed of our traditional cultural education system was to create a stereotyped image of us as

Figure 3.1 Cultural celebration of the marriage ritual: Breaking and sharing of kola nut and dry bush meat

Figure 3.2 Cultural celebration of the marriage ritual: Breaking and sharing of kola nut and dry bush meat

Figure 3.3 Funeral group

Figure 3.4 Funeral group

Figure 3.5 Funeral group

primitive people with primitive cultural practices. By so doing, the colonialists justified in their own minds the actions that they took to rupture and dislocate our customs and traditions regardless of the significance of these to all of our people.

The Christian missionaries sought to fulfil their mission of bringing about pious improvements to our lives. They aimed at providing as much at least as they thought was proportionate to the level of their own racial piety. So they introduced formal literary British education in our societies and in other West African societies through an offshoot of the evangelical and pietistic movements in the late eighteen and early nineteen centuries.

Such a system was therefore geared to producing trained personnel to administer the modern institutions and government establishments that they had established for their own interests and benefits.

In pursuance of this objective, those planning the curricular were very selective of the subjects that they included. However if altruism was any consideration in the planning of the curricula, it did not manifest in any regard for us, the natives, as compared with regard for the needs of the colonisers. If attention had been given to the meeting of our own needs, then achieving literacy in our own language and culture would have benefited our cultural heritage by preserving and perpetuating it through the system of literal record keeping. That would have extended the benefit of literal education for all our societies beyond the parameters of the British education system and our more insular system, which is limited by the characteristics of the oral traditional culture.

But the British colonialists' policy of deliberately dislocating our system marked yet another example of the subjugation of our citizens, enhancing a process that led to what amounts to amnesia, which obscures our memory of our origins and social networks, our roots and our heritage as a people. Nevertheless, that was the path that our colonisers took in their relationships with us.

Accordingly, starting from the more accessible coastal towns of Bathurst in Gambia, Accra in Gold Coast now Ghana, Lagos in 'Nigeria', and Free Town in Sierra Leone, as well as the Cape Coast, elementary and grammar schools were established. The wealthy people in these West African countries took the opportunity to educate their children at these institutions in our home countries and in the other West African countries and even at overseas institutions. From this group sprung an elite group of wealthy business men, lawyers, doctors, teachers, architects and ministers of religion. From this group also emerged the Black Victorians, whom I discussed in Chapter Two. Their demeaning of our traditions was followed by the resistance of another group in our society to what it saw as an attack on our culture.

In contrast to the Black Victorians, this group stood firm in its defence, determined to uphold the authenticity of the lives of our people and our right to observe and practice our traditional cultures, advocating for the establishment of an institution for the education of our natives in our various vernacular languages and the rehabilitation of West African cultural traditions and creative arts.

In the final analysis, the emergence of these two social groups is indirectly the result of the colonial missionaries' interventions in our societies as part of their attempts at converting us into Christianity.

The issue of our traditional religion encouraged people to think about the scenario of the colonial missionaries coming to our shores ostensibly to abolish the inhuman act of slave trade in our societies by converting us to Christianity. In order to do so successfully, they had to educate us and as a result there emerged the two social groups with two different reactions to British colonial education.

In the next chapter I will discuss the role of language and literature as an important element in the development of identity.

Note

1 In the 1960s, in light of the Synod for Africa, Second Vatican Council, there was an official change in the attitude of the Catholic church to non-Christian religions, including ATR. This followed two Synods for Africa.

Reference list

Achebe, C. (1958) *Things Fall Apart*. Oxford: Heinemann.
Achebe, C. (1960) *No Longer at Ease*. Oxford: Heinemann.
Achebe, C. (1964a) *The Arrow of God*. Oxford: Heinemann.
Achebe, C. (1964b) 'The role of the writer in the new nation', *Nigeria Magazine*, 81(June), pp. 157–160.
Achebe, C. (2001) *Home and Exile*. New York: Anchor Books, A Division of Random House Inc.
Coleman, J.S. (1958) *Nigeria: Background to Nationalism*. Berkeley and Los Angeles: University of California Press.
Conton, W. (1960) *The African*. London: Heinemann.
Crowder, M. (1962) *The Story of Nigeria*. London: Faber & Faber.
Diagne, P. (1967) *Pouvoir Politique traditional en Afrique Occidentale: essais sur les institutions Politiques précoloniales*. Paris: Présence Africaine.
Ekwensi, C. (1963) 'Problems of Nigerian writers', *Nigerian Magazine*, 78(September), pp. 217–219.
Erikson, E.H. (1968) *Identity, Youth & Crisis*. London: Faber & Faber.
Foulkes, S.H. (1964) *Therapeutic Group Analysis*. London: George Allen & Unwin Ltd.
Gaarder, J. (1995) *Sophie's World: An Adventure in Philosophy*. Translated by P. Moller. London: Pheonix House.
Isizoh, C.D. (2001) 'Dialogue with African traditional religion in Sub-Sahara Africa: The changing attitude of the catholic church', Christianity in Dialogue With African Traditional Religions and Culture. Seminar Papers, 1, pp. 1–42.
Johnston, H. (1930) *History of Colonisation of Africa, Alien Races*. Cambridge: Cambridge University Press.

Le Roy, J. (1987) 'The cultural structuring of the personality & intercultural relationship', *Group Analysis*, 20, pp. 147–153.

Le Roy, J. (1994) 'Group analysis & culture', in D. Brown and L. Zinkin eds., *The Psyche & the Social World*. London: Routledge.

Levtzion, N. (1973) *Ancient Ghana and Mali*. London: Methuen.

Mbiti, J. (1969) *African Religions and Philosophy*. London: Heinemann.

Obiechina, E. (1975) *Culture, Tradition and Society in the West African Novel*. African Studies Series 14. Cambridge: Cambridge University Press.

Paul VI. (1964) *Ecclesiam suam*. 6 August, Papal Encyclical Letter.

Pius X1. (1926) *Rerum Ecclesiae*. 28 February, Papal Encyclical Letter.

Soyinka, W. (1965) *The Interpreter*. London: A. Deutsch.

Chapter 4

The connections between language as one of our important cultural attributes and the development of identity

A people's language is one of the most important aspects of their culture. Our languages are to us as other people's are to them: means of verbal communications of speech and learning. As psychotherapists in a multicultural society we are used to working with people who have a wide variety of verbal modes of expression.

The language that we use to express our views, feelings and experiences, such as in the writing of this book, has great significance to our human relationships and interactions. Language is a means by which we can identify the culture of a people and their nationality – that is, their origin or ethnicity, or race.

(These words as I use them here are sociological constructions and are interchangeable in the sense that I use them here).

Aspects of the language of our West African people consist of physical gesticulations, such as various movements of the arms, facial expressions, shrugs of the shoulders, all of which in most of these societies give varying degrees of emphasis to aspects of communication. The manner of speaking, such as in proverbs, is also an important component of our language.

'Proverbs' as important components of our traditional languages

Proverbs, like gestures and facial movements, are particularly effective in conveying specific meanings and emphasis. Obiechina (1975) pointed out that to use proverbs is to put speech in traditional context, reinforcing personal points of view by objectifying its validity and indirectly paying tribute to oneself as a possessor of traditional wisdom.

There is a criticism of the use of proverbs, particularly of Achebe's in his novels, suggesting that the fact that proverbs appear so frequently is due to Achebe's characteristic fondness of their use rather than to the value of proverbs as a natural way of representing the linguistic reality of the world of rural novels.

However, proverbs form part of the speech of all our traditional societies and prose writers, whose characters are more of the oral than the literal, tend to write in a manner that is characterised by wise comments, full of proverbial lore.

In other words, proverbs are for the predominantly oral traditional cultures like ours, the *seed* which contains our wisdom.

According to Obiechina, they are philosophical and moral expositions, shrunk to a few words. They form a mnemonic device that helps the memory to retain everything that is worth knowing and that is relevant to the day-to-day life and therefore has to be committed to memory. Our societies find that by nature, proverbs perform an ideological function in that they make available the ideas and values that are encapsulated in the memorable and easily accessible '*seeds*' that they are.

They represent a collection of detailed observations of the behaviour of human beings and the entire system of thought and feeling that represents the collective views of society. These include observations of animals, plants and natural phenomena, beliefs, attitudes of the people, their feelings and even their way of thinking. Thus, when an individual member of society uses proverbs he, by implication, enacts one more way of demonstrating the primacy of the society. I would argue that by the same token it highlights the value of the language of a society as an important aspect of its culture.

Any social circumstance that is detrimental to a people's language is detrimental to an important aspect of the social institution of the society. That is why, I would argue, that the colonialists' ruling policies contained elements that ruptured and dislocated our social institutions and traditional cultures. Yet individual members of our societies place great value on this aspect of our traditional cultures. The corollary of this is a demonstration of the affinity between our culture and our identity as a people. By using proverbial languages, the traditional individuals of our society indicate their attachments to the community and its linguistic climate. It is not intended as means of expressing distinctiveness from the rest of the people of his society, by the traditional user; rather it is to indicate his attachment. This understanding of the nature of proverbs as part of our culture should emphasise the effectiveness of the efforts of our West African writers who used them to emphasise important points about our social life.

I would argue that it is legitimate to credit their efforts with great effectiveness since they were in position to write in the languages of our people's very own constructions.

For all these reasons, I consider the issue of language to be particularly pertinent to this book since its main aspects concern expressing and transmitting the characteristic behaviours of two different societies with their different cultural traditions, namely the British colonialists and ours.

The words that make up our language are themselves culturally bound and our languages are one of the major aspects of our cultures, a significant part of it. In any situation like ours, when and where they fail to serve us in the understanding of our social culture, we can rightly assume that this may be because we have entered a different social environment from our familiar ones. Where there exist differences in the languages used by a group of people it would be reasonable to assume that the group is made up of people of more than one culture because language is a definite cultural identity; it is peculiar to the culture of its origin.

That is why and how the intervention in our culture by the British with their language had a detrimental effect to us in more ways than one. To be in a position to be able to communicate only in a foreign language when I am outside the confines of my own particular native society makes me to feel alienated from my real self, especially when others who are not members of my society treat my own language with contempt. To be able to speak only in the foreign language of my colonisers makes me to feel continually under colonisation and in this case by the foreign language.

As Frantz Fanon (1967) stated about the significance of language, being colonised by a language has significant implications for one's consciousness. 'To speak . . . means above all to assume a culture, to support the right of a civilisation'. Speaking a language which is foreign to one's culture means that one accepts or is coerced into accepting the collective consciousness of the foreigner whose language is being spoken. In the cases of those of us who were educated in English literacy and spoke it, this implied that we accepted the collective consciousness of the British. In reality we were reacting to what we had been forced to accept. This brings me to an important element in the development of my own identity: understanding and coming to terms with the language of Western group psychotherapy.

The language of group psychotherapy

In the psychotherapy and group analytic culture, for example, one of the most vital factors that come into the process of the training and clinical practice is the state of the unconscious 'mind' of the patient or client as well as that of the therapist.

The word consciousness refers to the state of awareness of one's self and one's surroundings. It has derivatives showing different degrees of intensity to which it can manifest the state of awareness as, for example, being in semi-consciousness, sub-consciousness or pre-consciousness state.

It would be reasonable to assume that both patients or clients and the therapists would be familiar with the meaning of these words and the context in which they are used. Yet, the word 'consciousness' and its derivatives are not part of the repertoire of the Igbo languages, for example. That is to say that there are no words in the Igbo languages that are equivalent to them; they do not include the words conscious, consciousness, sub-consciousness, or pre-consciousness in any sense as part of the phenomena of the state of the human mind. There is no concept of the meaning of these words as they are used in the psychotherapeutic sense in the Western traditions.

The sense in which the state of unawareness of the self or unconsciousness comes into the Igbo usage or custom is quite different from the psychotherapeutic and group analytic understanding of the human mind and the consequences of that understanding to human behaviours and affective reactions. Whereas the psychotherapeutic and group analytic use of those words relates to feelings and states of the human 'mind', an abstract entity, the Igbo language sense in which the words consciousness or unconsciousness come into usage and custom is in conditions not related to such abstract entity as the 'mind'. It is rather in relation to the activity of the physical and visibly palpable human anatomy: the heart.

The state of unconsciousness is not understood in relation to the state in which dreams occur as in the mind or the state in which thoughts and pictures, for example, occur in people's minds. Thoughts and pictures are referred to here to elaborate further the identifying characteristics and meaning of the word 'mind' in the psychotherapeutic sense.

In explaining the words 'conscious', 'semi-conscious', 'sub-conscious', and 'unconscious' as used in the European psychotherapeutic or group analytic sense, I have had to use the word 'mind' as the subject that these other words 'conscious', 'semi-conscious' or 'unconscious' qualify. The word being abstract and inanimate is therefore to be understood here as elsewhere, as existing in a metaphysical sense. That is, it is not available to touch, it is not palpable. But it is assigned a power or force for thinking and perception.

The Igbos would not understand the meaning of the word 'mind' in the sense that Europeans in general and European psychotherapists in particular do. But they would understand the processes of the power of the 'mind' where those powers are attributed to the forces of the palpable human 'heart' instead of the abstract mind.

In other words, there is no conception of an existence of the 'mind' which has the power and force that the European language and culture attribute to it.

Similarly, when we use the words conscious, consciousness, unconsciousness, or pre-consciousness, in the Western sense, it is usually in relation to the force of the inanimate object – the 'mind'. There are, one is aware, occasions in our usage of words when we say for example, 'in your heart of hearts' meaning, according to what your heart feels or tells you. At other times we may say, 'do what your heart tells you', suggesting that the heart animates the mechanism of all those psychological states which we usually assign to the forces of the inanimate object the 'mind'.

In such instances, the Westerner will understand the same 'sense' made by the usage of the word 'heart' by the Igbos, even though the tangible object (the palpable organ) the 'heart' is assigned the power, and the force which the Western psychotherapy (as well as other Western cultures) normally assigns to the non-palpable and inanimate 'mind'.

The usage of language in Igbo as well as in Western culture when appropriately applied will be effective in conveying the desired meaning but they would be ineffective if, through ethnocentric prejudice, the affinity of language to its cultural origin is ignored. Evidence of the value of gesticulation and proverbs in the Igbo languages, illustrate the peculiarities of languages to their cultural origins

Consider therefore the situation of a student such as myself, whose first language is not English, and who – when already socially, culturally mature in his own native environment – finds himself immersed in the rigours of psychotherapy training in the Western European model, in pursuit of Western innovative training and modernism.

Vignette 4.1 Reflections on beginning group analysis

As I recall my experience of being immersed in Western psychotherapy training, I also recall some feelings regarding another instance in my life when I was searching for myself through the system of group analytic exploration. I recall now the feeling that eluded me on that occasion as I was exposed to the different mechanisms involved in the explorations of one's self through the Western methods of group analytic training and practice including the theoretical perspective, the personal group analysis perspective and the clinical group practice experiences. Although it was not compulsory for me to undertake this, I had been led to believe that it was the way forward for anyone aspiring to the lifestyle and behaviours that are considered to be more appropriate in the wider and more civilised communities of the world.

However, although the philosophy behind the idea of finding oneself through this Western method of group analysis claimed to be an innovative and a more civilised one, it was nevertheless strange and alien to me. It brought back the memories of the alienation from my natural heritage that I suffered as a result of the British colonial ruling policies.

It felt to me as if yet again I was alienated by the conspiracies of the different aspects of the mechanisms involved in the search for one's self through the group analytic processes and culture. It was as if I was in 'exile' again but this time within the group analytic community of White man's culture: a Black man and his Black culture in the midst of White man's culture which I had been trapped into seeking, believing it to be superior.

For me in particular, this increased my resolve to discover who I am, much as such an experience increased the resolve of all our societies to employ all means available to us as a people to redeem ourselves from our state of virtual bondage which had denied us our rights to enjoy our natural cultural identity as a people. By this I mean to live our lives in the way that we feel that we should; the way that our ancestors had done; and the way that had become customary to us as societies of human beings when we are not constrained through coercion.

The English language in which I was obliged to do my training as a group analyst was certainly a problem, especially as some of the otherwise ordinary English words acquire special meanings in the particular context of vocabularies used in psychotherapy. I felt very strange and alienated by these vocabularies; these were not just new and strange words, some of them were special words coined by psychologists for psychotherapists' use (Pines, 1987). It was particularly difficult to share the experiences of my training and practice in psychotherapy with my kinsmen in our Igbo society. Because of the problem of language, in terms of the words available to me, it was difficult even to explain to them as adequately as I felt that I needed to, what the practice of psychotherapy was about, without using the English language including the special words in which the training was conducted (Azu-Okeke, 1990).

I argue that there will always be a loss of some understanding and meaning in translating words from one culture to another, because every culture is unique and language is an integral part of a culture. It is an illusion for a person from one culture to think that he fully understands the language of people of a different culture. Such understanding can only be a matter of degree. There will always be something lost in translation.

In oral traditional cultures like those of my Igbo nation, for example, the beliefs, customs and rules are transmitted by word of mouth. The words themselves, however, have their origins in both the setting or environment in which they form the natural means of verbal expressions and communications, and in the factors which govern the naming of things, situations, events and occasions in such societies.

The labelling and identification of different things in our social environments, whether things physical or metaphysical, things visible or invisible to the senses, or occasions such as performances of cultural rites in the societies are contingent on many and different factors in the societies. Some things are given their names according to how they are used and those names become peculiar to the things that they name, and to the particular society which names them as such. The words on these name-labels become organised into the language of the people. A nation of people can then be identified by their language. It is natural and easier to express emotions, for example, in one's own native language.

Some years ago the issue of understanding the role of people's cultures in their reactions to stressful conditions of life took its toll among the African and African/Caribbean mental ill health patients who were in psychiatric hospitals to receive treatments. This was because their behaviours and manners of reactions and responses were often misunderstood and sadly gave cause to misdiagnoses of their problems and consequently wrongly influenced their treatment regimes, clearly a result of ignorance about the importance to all people of their natural means of expressing themselves.

This can give rise to the situation that Littlewood and Lipsedge (1982) dealt with in their book, *Aliens and Alienists: Ethnic minorities and psychiatry*. They assessed the psychological consequences of migration and prejudice for such diverse groups as West Indians, Turkish Cypriots and Hasidic Jews. They examined the epidemiology of mental ill health among ethnic minorities and Black Britons, using a combination of psychiatric and social anthropological theoretical perspectives.

They came to the conclusion that mental illness can be an intelligible response to disadvantage and prejudice. I would argue, however, that the behaviours of the Afro-Caribbean and West Africa people (the ethnic minorities and blacks), seen as 'strange and unusual', are often misunderstood considered in the context of Western culture. Consequently the motive behind the behaviour is misinterpreted and often results in it being 'pathologised' as a manifestation of psychiatric problems. In other words the psychiatrist defends against his ignorance of the cultural behaviours which are different from his by using some psychiatric theoretical perspective to label the minority group.

My argument is that much too often this is what happens and that highlights the importance of any aspect of a people's culture such as their language, suggesting that even where it is a barrier in communication, it should not be defended against by some ethnocentric cultural bias. I would argue that seeing things only from the point of view of one's own culture and ignoring the evidence of the importance of a different culture which needs to be addressed is a practice of ethnocentric prejudice.

Littlewood and Lipsedge's argument is that ethnic minority groups can find mental illness 'an intelligible response to disadvantage and prejudice'. In my view they are saying that mental illness, in such instance, serves the ethnic minority group as a defence against the disadvantages of belonging to a racial minority group and also defence against prejudicial behaviours to which they often feel subjected.

The lingua franca

The language of a culture shared by all its members becomes their 'lingua franca'. Although it can be also used by non-natives who have learned to use it, it belongs to those who in the first place made up the words that are articulated to form the lingua franca. Therefore the language forms part of the people's cultural identity as indeed our languages were to us when they were abused and denigrated by the colonial ruling policies. They remain still important aspects of our culture.

Yet the British colonial education policy treated and held our native languages in contempt and therefore omitted and neglected literacy in them. In their stead, we were coerced into accepting the collective consciousness of the British who identified our blackness with inferiority as one feels had been characteristic of most European cultures. That in effect implied that we too identified ourselves with inferiority by being coerced into looking down on our languages and omitting literacy education in them.

The only languages that were included in the curricula in any serious sense were English and other languages such as French, German, Latin and even Greek.

If the British colonialists' reason for not including the native languages in our education curricular was due to an inability to organise teaching them, one wonders what their reason was for actively discouraging their being recognised and respected as important aspect of a people's culture. Evidently they recognised enough of the importance of language to persist on preserving it by even coercing us to learn it. On the other hand, to demonstrate their racial prejudice they demeaned our own languages and encouraged us to demean them too. Thus our languages suffered racial prejudicial treatment by being relegated to the bottom of the hierarchy of languages as 'mumbo jumbo' of primitive people with primitive cultures, done out of racial prejudice and the determination to focus their attention on the exploitation of our natural resources.

Frantz Fanon (1967) stated that 'Western bourgeois racial prejudice as regards the nigger (the black man) and the Arab is a racism of contempt; it is a racism which minimises what it hates'.

The colonialists did not show appreciable interest in our native languages either for their own personal need, as a means to improve the relationship between them and us (the natives), nor for the benefit of the natives in order that we might benefit from the literacy of reading and writing in our own mother tongues. However, to its credit, the knowledge of literacy which the British education gave to us broke the psychic insularity that is characteristic of our traditional system of education. In addition the more that we as a people learned such a cosmopolitan language as English, the more that we were equipped with a common language that served all those of us who could hitherto not communicate inter-stately because of course we had and spoke our different languages. Also, as I said earlier, we lived mostly within the confines of our own different native societies.

But following some English education, those of us who had previously spoken only our own native language learned to speak and even to write the English language and were able to communicate more widely at inter-state levels. As Obiechina (1975) again observed, this literacy in the English language 'encouraged greater physical mobility and consequently the broadening of the social as well as psychological outlook'.

Still, I would argue that overall the British education policy was another example of the calculated strategies of the colonialists to humiliate, stagnate, disorganise and demoralise us.

People's language is one of their greatest cultural heritages and, as such, it is a source of great pride to the people, an index of their identity profile by which they can project themselves as a people.

Our native writers who did much to project the values of our cultural heritages were able to do so only in the English language because they lacked the literacy education in our native languages. There were, however, efforts made to achieve a degree of literacy in some of these and that enabled some communications in the vernacular.

Alas this group of our nationalists, who had the courage to attempt to write for us in our native languages, were discouraged by mockery of their efforts both by some of our natives encouraged by the colonisers, as well as by the colonisers themselves directly. But the saddest and most painful aspect of this situation was that our own people, such as the Black Victorians, were coerced to condescend to betraying their own native cultures through this particular important aspect of it, our language.

The fact that it was possible for this situation to occur is testimony to the degree of effectiveness of the colonialist coercions and indoctrinations of our minds.

The saying that 'literacy mediates between the novelist, writer and the reader and makes the rapport possible' became only partially true because of the omission of teaching us our own rich native languages. In teaching English, the colonialists used English idioms and words that arose from English social life experiences, peculiar only to English culture and traditions. Nevertheless, natives like myself were taught to use such words to describe things and situations belonging to our own societies, for example, society, tribe, clan, village, because these were the most approximate to what the colonialists wished to describe and express to us.

Psychotherapy culture makes many assumptions of languages that belong solely for its use and excludes those who are not within its fraternity. It has an ideology of its own which guides it to set its standards and values and the principles for training and practising. The language and culture are usually of the middle-class Europeans and therefore excludes people of lower social class. This highlights another aspect of language as a cross-cultural issue that affects our social interactions.

Following our British education based on these vocabularies we use these words in reference to our native situations and circumstances. We feel obliged to use them as the British or British educated teachers teach us to do and in some instances because the White people 'who know best' say so. Even today because our literacy education omitted to include our native languages we had no opportunity to learn to write in our own vocabularies constructed according to the rules by which we as a culture developed them. Our native languages were not developed according to the British contexts for constructing words and vocabularies, naming objects, situations and describing circumstances in and out of our environments.

The context in which the formulation of words has developed in different societies of the world is an important factor that, in my view, Leslie Swartz (1998) clarified in his explanation of the 'universal theorists' approaches to understanding mental health and mental illness. Swartz explained that the fundamental assumption of universalism is that mental illness is universal. The task then is to find evidence for these universals. Two things may obscure the true nature of universal illness; one of these is the way that we name conditions in different settings and the other is how conditions are expressed in different cultures. The central issues here are, one, a 'given', in this case mental illness which in one setting may be seen as an affliction of the devil in those societies that believe in the metaphysical causation of illness in spite of an existence of evidence of a head injury that should be considered as a possible cause of the problem. While in another society that believes in organic causality of illness, they would consider the possibility of organic causality of the illness.

Swartz also cited an example in which Leff (1988), in his introduction of his book on trans-cultural psychiatry, tells the story of two butterfly collectors, one in Britain and the other in 'Nigeria'. The British collector has discovered a butterfly that he called the 'Battersea Beauty' and the Nigerian collector discovered one that he called the 'Ibadan Imperial'. Following correspondences, the two collectors found that although they had both been using different words to describe the butterflies, they had found examples of the same butterfly. That means that they had been talking about the same thing but using different words. The British collector lived in a culture in which there is a local environment called Battersea where he discovered a species of butterfly which the Nigerian collector found in a place in Nigeria called Ibadan. The British collector could not be expected to name the butterfly that he discovered the Ibadan Imperial, any more than the Nigerian collector could have called the butterfly that he discovered in Nigeria the Battersea Beauty. The deciding factor in each of these cases is the different cultural environments in which these collectors lived and had their experiences of ecology.

In the quest for epistemology, Immanuel Kant according to Ted Benton (1977) also argued that the basis for knowledge of the world is innate in all mankind and universal. Our experience of the world around us or our environment is made out of syntheses of the world we encounter and which forms our conceptual frame of our world outside our self.

There is a distinction between things as they are and things as they appear to us – the 'noumena' and the 'phenomena', respectively, and our experience of things as they are to us is the 'phenomena' according to Kant. That is why different cultures have different names for the same things that exist in their respective cultural environments. Hence different cultures have their own different languages.

One of our eminent writers, Chinua Achebe (2001), pointed to a particular case in point regarding the use of words according to their English meaning to apply to a different culture as if the words should have the same value in describing or explaining the same thing in the different social environments. He gave as an example the use of the word 'tribe' to describe the social status of the Igbo people. Achebe pointed out that according to the Pocket Oxford dictionary, the characteristics that were attributed to the Igbos as a tribe of people by the Western writers were actually the characteristic status of a 'nation' of people, rather than of a 'tribe' of people.

In order to express our rich culture in its original form, it would have been best to do so in our first language. However, that is not to be mainly because of my lack of adequate literacy education in my Igbo language, as this was neglected in my education. Even if I were educated in literacy in my native language and so able to write this book in the Igbo language, the readers would have had to have received literal education in the Igbo language in order to be able to read it. It is my belief that British scholars did not avail themselves of the opportunity to learn the Igbo language.

The birth of national policy on our language education

I have argued frequently here that there was reluctance on the part of our colonisers for us to engage with much interest in education in our various native languages. (There are about five hundred 'Nigerian' languages.) I have also argued about how our colonisers added to this act of omission the devaluation of our native languages as 'mumbo jumbo'.

Here I aim to present another perspective to the issue of our education in our languages.

According to Taiwo (1980) and Fafunwa (1974), there were early efforts made in at least some parts of our societies to engage in our native language education. I will consider the outcome of those efforts in the particular context of the cultural value of a people's language to them and therefore the implications for the integrity of the people's identity if and when that aspect of their culture is dislocated and ruptured. Although formal Western-type education was introduced into the country by Christian missionaries just before the middle of the nineteenth century, since then until after about four decades had elapsed after that initial date, both the nature and main thrust of language education in the country were completely left to those missionaries to decide.

The beliefs of most of such missionaries apparently were well known to be first, that the African child was best taught in his native language (Hair, 1967) and, second, that the interests of Christianity would best be served by actually propagating that religion in indigenous languages. Accordingly, the teaching and learning of indigenous languages received much genuine attention in those early days of Western-type education in the country.

But this approach was short lived, not being whole heartedly liked or approved, as the products of such a system of education were thought not to be well suited to the job market of those days, in which the unsatisfied needs were for persons with training in English rather than in the indigenous languages. According to Taiwo (1980), members of the then elite were widely of the view that the people turned out under that system of education were not suitable.

I believe that it is reasonable to question the motive for giving education; what interest is meant to be served. It seems to me to be an action plan that follows the aims and purposes of colonialism – that is, using exploitative means available to them to acquire the natural resources that they required. From then on, the education system was geared strictly to producing people to serve as teachers, clerks, preachers, all the cadre of people that they required for their new establishments; as their sole motive for educating the natives was utilitarian, English language was accorded a lot more prominence in this system of education.

Over time, that policy succeeded so well that interest in language education in the country shifted substantially away from the indigenous languages towards English, the language of the colonial masters. Proof of this was the following: first, pupils and their parents gradually formed the opinion that it was financially more rewarding to study English than any of the indigenous languages; second, certification became conditional upon passing English; and, finally, the various governments in the country from the colonial times till well past the attainment of political independence in 1960, rarely felt that they had any duty to promote the study of the indigenous languages, whereas they considered themselves obliged to encourage and even enforce the study of English.

Luckily, as only few indigenous school children, if any at all, in those days, spoke any English before actually entering school, such children therefore willy-nilly had to be instructed in the medium of their mother tongues, until they had gained enough proficiency in English by their fourth, fifth or even sixth year in school to be able to receive all or most formal instruction in it.

However, even up to this stage, the mother tongue existed as an optional subject on the curriculum, particularly in the case of those languages like Efik, Hausa, Igbo and Yoruba that were lucky enough not only to have been reduced to writing but to also have sufficient reading materials both sacred and secular for use in teaching school children.

After the attainment of political independence in 1960, the wisdom of giving English so much importance in Government and Education began gradually to be questioned. As a result of this new development, people openly canvassed in the seats of government for English to be replaced as the official language by one of our indigenous languages. That, according to Bamgbose (1976), was some twenty years after independence. Others who were particularly worried by the problem most people in the country actually have in understanding English and communicating well in it, advised that more effort should be put into the teaching of the major indigenous languages to enable them to serve as an alternative to English as official means of communication in Government and Business (Osaji, 1979, quoting the White Paper on the Udoji Report).

This is the degree to which people's consciousness had been awakened to the threat to part of our cultural heritage, our languages, our means of communications, the means by which we educate our children. The lobbyists were effective and succeeded in bringing enough pressure to force what became an important shift in the attitude of the Government, particularly at the Federal level, to the indigenous languages.[1]

The effect of this shift was in the first instance a form of an admission by Government of what had long been known to linguists and anthropologists, namely that a language is simultaneously a vehicle for a people's culture and a means of maintaining and indefinitely preserving that culture. The implication of this, which Government came to see and appreciate, is that if we are not ultimately to lose our national identity together with our rich indigenous cultures, then we must begin to pay more attention to the teaching of our indigenous languages.

In addition to seeing the relationship between language and culture, the Government also came to see the indigenous languages more clearly for what they had been all along: a veritable and practical means of communication, some of which could very easily be harnessed for effecting national integration, a matter of paramount importance for a country still struggling to consolidate its independence.

There is certainly a good basis for concluding that the present state of our language education in our societies today, as compared to its state at the turn of the last century, has shown much progress during that intervening period. The purpose of highlighting the many problems currently besetting particularly the teaching of English and the indigenous languages in our schools today is to lay the basis for further or future progress in that order and at the same time provide a sort of reference point against which to meet or assess such progress.

There is reason to feel optimistic about recovering this aspect of our cultural heritage. Yet one longs for the time when, as in some other world communities that hold dear the value of their cultural heritage, we can forge ahead and recover this aspect of our culture especially at this time in our history when we ourselves ostensibly hold the reins of power in our societies.

It would be such a great achievement to emulate what happened in the United Kingdom regarding the indigenous languages of Ireland, Scotland and Wales. These languages are taught and anyone wanting to work in Wales needs to learn Welsh. All their official documents have to be translated from Welsh for whoever needs to know the contents. The Nigerian official documents are an open English book, as it were, in their master's voice.

Concluding thoughts

It is an inescapable human condition that what we are psychologically is a function of our root from where we have grown up and are moulded or fashioned as human beings. This symbiotic relationship can be such that it can be said of a person that he or she behaves like a West African, for example, or an English man, or a Welsh man, or of any other country based on the known cultural characteristics of such societies. This is because each of them has its imprint, which it leaves on those who develop within their sphere of influence and that a keen eye of an observer with knowledge of the characteristics of such society can detect, because certain cultural characteristics are peculiar to certain societies.

For example, in the Abiriba Igbo society, the child is named after someone living or who has died and believed to have gone onto spirit world, which takes place on the eighth day after the birth, is an important cultural rite from which the child grows up to see the evidence of and identify himself or herself with as evidence of his or her cultural identity.

This is a cultural belief that has an effect on the formation of the child's identity, for the child is constantly and proudly informed of the person for whom he or she has been named. In our type of society the extended relationship with a great person who has passed on from this life enters into the child's perception of his or her persona and therefore of the image of himself or herself that he or she projects to others.

Names have meanings in the language of the society that gives such names, and language, as I have argued is culturally bound. This very issue of name and culture of origin was one of the issues that created conflict between us the natives and the colonial missionaries who always insisted on giving us names that have no relevance to our traditional cultures. Nor do the meanings of the foreign names that they insist on calling us at our baptism relate to anything about our culture nor have any meaningful significance to the individual, to the parents who give names in honour of an important person of the society according to our social-cultural traditions.

In the realms of psychotherapy and group analysis, ego development and individuation are important and prominent since they are issues of development of identity. It is therefore significant that Sigmund Freud's approach to 'ego' development, which he argued was motivated by the child's need to satisfy his sexual need, was considered to have important shortcomings by ignoring the value of relationship with 'others'. In other words by ignoring the value of the social network. The 'Object relations' theorists including Fairbairn (1952), Guntrip (1969), Winnicott (1965), Balint (1975) argued that the primary motivational drive in man is to seek relationship with others. Hence it is the natural process for the individual to seek relationship with others beginning at first with the mother/caregiver.

When the social and political policies of the colonialists ruptured and dislocated the cohesiveness of our social-cultural structure, individuals were at the risk of becoming disorientated and alienated from their natural 'self' and identity because, we could no longer develop according to our autochthon root, we could no longer be sure of who we were, or how to describe ourselves and claim the basis for being human beings. We now have the task of rescuing our future from the ravages of colonialism. I am aware that this will not be an easy task; on the contrary it is an onerous task that faces us. There are questions that we need to answer arising from our experiences of the colonial rule such as 'What would we have become if the root of our cultural traditions had not been so indifferently, indeed so nonchalantly dislocated and ruptured that we lost our social bearing and direction as societies?'

I argue strongly that there is a close relationship between our roots, that is our social-cultural traditional practices and our identity as a people. I argue also that through their system of administration of our societies' coercions, degradations and subjugations culminating in what I have termed 'psychic colonisation', the colonialists deprived us of, and alienated us from the substances of our cultural heritage and in effect, we were deprived of our identity.

In discussing these three aspects of our cultural traditions in this chapter, namely our languages, our traditional system of education and our traditional religious beliefs, my aim has been to show some of the impact of the colonisers' culture on us the colonised people.

Having arrived at this juncture of knowing the source of my afflictions, so to say, I am now left in that position in which I feel that I know where I am and so can plot where I am going. However, Karl Marx had left us with a conundrum to consider regarding this juncture in our lives when he warned that philosophers might have interpreted the world; what remains, however, is how to change it.

Now that I know where the colonial heritage has placed us, I shall discuss my thoughts on our future in my final chapters. Firstly, however, in Chapter Five I shall acknowledge the contribution made to this book by my follow Igbos, and how their own reflections on the impact of colonialism on their lives helped me to better understand how our identity has been affected, through different generations, from my peers (the elders) through to the younger generation who did not directly experience colonial rule.

Note

1   The Federal Government of Nigeria began from the late 1970s onward to take official interest in, and make policy pronouncements on the teaching of the indigenous languages, instead of concerning itself solely with English as hitherto. Thus, in an official document that was first published in 1977 and revised in 1981 by the title of Federal Republic of Nigeria National Policy on Education (NPE), the Federal Government for the first time laid down as a policy for the whole country that:

   a   in primary School, which lasts six years, each child must study two languages, namely:

   i   his mother-tongue (if available for study) or an indigenous language of wider communication in his area of domicile, and

   ii   English language;

   b   in Junior Secondary School (JSS), which is of three years' duration, the child must study three languages, viz:

   i   his mother-tongue (if available for study) or an indigenous language of wider communication in his area of domicile,

ii English language, and
iii just any one of the three major indigenous language in the country, namely Hausa, Igbo, and Yoruba, provided the Language chosen is distinct from the child's mother-tongue;

c in Senior Secondary School (SSS), which also lasts three years, the child must study two languages, viz:

i an indigenous language, and
ii English language

Reference list

Achebe, C. (2001) *Home & Exile*. New York: Anchor Books.

Azu-Okeke, O. (1990) *Implications of Social and Psychological Factors for Group Analytic Psychotherapy Treatment of the Igbo People of the S.E. Central Nigeria*. Unpublished Manuscript.

Balint, M. (1975) *The Doctor, His Patient and the Illness*. New York: International University Press.

Bamgbose, A. (1976) 'Language in national integration: Nigeria as a case study', Read at the 12th W. African Language Congress, University of Ife, Ife, Nigeria, March 15–20.

Benton, T. (1977) *Philosophical Foundations of the Three Sociologies*. London: Routledge & Kegan Paul.

Fafunwa, A.B. (1974) *History of Education in Nigeria*. London: George Allen & Unwin, p. 92.

Fairbairn, W.R.D. (1952) *An Object-Relations Theory of the Personality*. London: Tavistock Publications.

Fanon, F. (1967) *Black Skin White Mask*. Translated by C.L. Markmann. New York: Grove Press.

Guntrip, H. (1969) *Schizoid Phenomena: Object-Relations and the Self*. New York: International University Press.

Hair, P.E.H. (1967) *The Early Study of Nigerian Languages: Essays and Bibliographies*. London: Cambridge University Press.

Leff, J. (1988) *Psychiatry Around the Globe: A Transcultural View*. 2nd edition. New York: Marcel Dekker.

Littlewood, R. and Lipsedge, M. (1982) *Aliens and Alienists: Ethnic Minorities and Psychiatry*. London: Penguin.

Obiechina, E. (1975) *Culture, Tradition and Society in the West African Novel*. African Studies Series 14. Cambridge: Cambridge University Press.

Osaji, B. (1979) *Language Survey in Nigeria*. Publication B-81. Quebec: International Centre for Research of Bilingualism.

Pines, M. in Cox, M. and Theilgaard, A. (1987) *Mutative Metaphors in Psychotherapy: The Aeolian Mode*. London: Tavistock Publications.

Swartz, L. (1998) *Culture and Mental Health: A South African View*. Cape Town: Oxford University Press.

Taiwo, C.O. (1980) *The Nigerian Education System*. Lagos: Thomas Nelson (Nigeria) Ltd., pp. 10–11.

Winnicott, D.W. (1965) *The Maturational Process and the Facilitating Environment*. New York: International Press.

Chapter 5

Talking to my peers
The importance of shared experiences

In this chapter I will draw on the reflections from earlier chapters and explain how I set about contacting and subsequently interviewing other Igbo people, who were of a similar age group and thus had experience of colonialism first-hand, and some younger people for whom it was a 'done deal' so to speak. I will include a brief account of the methodological framework I used for this part of the book – namely autoethnography, ethnography and narrative, together with some details of how I contacted potential participants to complete a questionnaire and later participate in a discussion with myself or as part of a group.

My book has set out to explore the effects of the British colonial ruling policies for us, as Igbo people, during their occupation. As far as I know this is a unique area of enquiry into the social phenomena of the people of Igboland and the other societies in West Africa that the British colonial rulers included in what they eventually named the country of Nigeria. It is unique in that it is written by someone who grew up at this time and was obliged to live within two very different and often clashing cultures, leading to some serious trauma and conflict of identity, which I have described in Chapter One under the story of the bird-shooting rite of passage and its celebration, Igba Nnunu and Ignu Nnunu, respectively. In the planning of the book and the research which underpins it, I have had to take into consideration our origin and evolution as a society of Igbo people, looking at celebrations of rites of passage, categories of groups of affiliations – uke – and oral traditional face-to-face interactions, which are relatively more homogeneous than in a literate culture.

In order to manage what felt like an overwhelming task, I set about identifying a research method that would enable me to organise my material for both my and the reader's sake. In this chapter, I outline the methodology I used to gain as much relevant data as possible to support my own position on the merits or otherwise of the colonial regime. An important aspect of this data gathering concerned eliciting the views of Igbo people from a variety of different ages – those of my own age group who grew up under colonialism up to the younger generation who had no direct experience of it. Thus the focus of the research is on how the colonial regime might have affected the way that we, the autochthon members of our societies, lived our lives over that period of active colonialist occupation, against the background of the contrasting cultures of our societies and those of the British colonialists. It is also aimed at assessing our views about our life experiences under our self-governing periods as compared with our experiences under the colonial regime. In other words, how we saw ourselves and our lives before colonialism, during, and after it.

I approached research for the book through a qualitative heuristic inquiry methodology because, as Clark Moustakas (1990) wrote:

> Heuristic inquiry is a process that begins with a question or problem which the researcher seeks to illuminate or answer. The question is the one that has been a personal challenge and puzzlement in the search to understand oneself and the world in which one lives.

This applies to my circumstances, as I made clear when I discussed the author's perspectives in Chapter One. Also the heuristic process is autobiographic; that is, it is a story of one's own life, but at the same time it has a social and even universal significance.

It provides a way of engaging in scientific search through methods and processes that are aimed at discovering. It is a way of self-inquiry and dialogue with others that tries to discover the underlying meanings of important human experiences. In addition to the characteristics stated above, heuristic enquiry enabled me to be both a participant and an observer in my search, as I explored the different aspects of the lives and circumstances of the societies of which I am a member. At the heart of heuristics lies an emphasis on disclosing the self as a way of facilitating disclosure from others; a response of the tacit dimension within oneself sparks a similar call from others.

I was therefore in a position of self-dialogue in which I faced myself in the process of understanding my place in those societies. It is the task of my research to explore with myself as part of the subject of my explorations, and in order to do this, I had to be honest with myself because of my desire to come to terms with that part of myself which was yet a mystery to me, hence the subject of my ardent curiosity. In my research, I was about to embark on a journey of enquiring into all the possible circumstances of the lives of people of our societies, especially as it was my own personal desire to undertake this exploration in order to find answers to some inner conflicts which, like an unlaid ghost, would not rest until exorcised. Clark Moustakas (1990) argued that since heuristic inquiry utilises qualitative methodology in arriving at themes and essences of experiences, validity in heuristics is not a matter of quantitative measurement that can be determined by correlation or statistics. Rather, determination of validity is a matter of whether the ultimate depiction of the experience derived from one's own rigorous, exhaustive self-searching presents comprehensively, vividly and accurately the meaning and essence of the experience. It is also a matter of whether the experiences of others involved also depict comprehensively, vividly and accurately the meaning and essence of their experiences.

Another advantage of using heuristic inquiry is that it seeks to discover the meaning of phenomena and to elicit meaning from direct first person accounts of individuals who have experienced these. Hence it will then be appropriate for me to involve group participation in which people will be asked to bring up their personal experiences of life during and after colonialism.

Using this methodology, I followed three main approaches to collecting data:

1 Acquiring information of a socio-historical and political nature derived from official documents, fiction and non-fiction, questionnaires and interviews.
2 Autoethnographical enquiry – derived from my own experience as a child growing up in two different cultures and the impact that had on my life and my choices.
3 Narrative enquiry – stories derived from interviews, personal recollections of those living in colonial times and shortly afterwards.

The socio-historical and political perspective

I have explored the nature of the social lives of our West African societies before the British colonialists arrived, giving an insight to the social atmosphere that I suggest was dislocated and disrupted by British colonial policies. This perspective also allowed for an examination of the psycho-social aspects of the lives of people of essentially two diverse cultures. To aid this enquiry I collected information from sources such as interviews, questionnaires and, as I mentioned earlier, data from group interactions including from members of our older generations who have a history of long and varied experiences of social life in our societies. This gives legitimacy to recalling memories of historical facts of our societies acquired as legacies bequeathed to us by our ancestors. As Robin Higgins argued, when we begin a journey of exploration, our steps may move outwards into the world about us, or inwardly into our memories and experiences or more usually, in both directions simultaneously or successively.

Ethnographical perspective including autoethnography

It became clear as I developed my studies, that my inquiry was and is about who we are, the Igbo people, and who I am myself, the enquirer, especially as I was born into two cultures that militated against one another. I came to believe that the way to my discovering who we are and in particular who I am, involves the task of ethnology. I was then able to explore, to begin with, the various contours and subdivisions of units of our families, our origins, our characteristics as races of people, our physical and linguistic classifications.

I believe that these observations enabled me to make adequate and appropriate assessments and conclusions about the changes that the dislocations and rupturing of our social and cultural institutions by the colonial policies have caused our societies.

Equally, it will show any benefits to us that might have resulted from the same colonial ruling policies. Through an ethnological perspective, I explored different aspects of our social-cultural lives and also considered those of the British, judging from their attitudes toward us as one of their colonised societies. This ethnographical approach enabled me to understand more fully the impact of the colonisers' ruling policies on the ego development of our children and our cultural identity as a people. I feel that this is particularly relevant to our societies that are characterised by a culture of social groups of affiliations. The ethnological perspective took into account the impact of language as an important part of our culture and how being forced to abandon our respective native languages for the alien English language of our colonisers affected members of our societies; and how the acquisition of British literate education also meant the loss of some of our native cultural attributes, given that language is culturally bound. Also explored were the origins of our traditional religions, and those of the colonialists, and of the colonised West African societies, which in some aspects are antithetical to that of the colonisers.

The narrative approach

This approach was central as a tool for collecting information that included the author's personal experiences of the colonial regime in his own Igbo native societies and the conflicts that arose for me because of the nature of the colonialists' ruling policies. Also the consequences of those conflicts on the pattern of my social interactions, especially the problems that arose for me during my formative years and the implications for my future life aspirations.

The narrative perspective has provided the tool to tell the story of our people's experiences of these policies. It is also an appropriate tool for exploring the roles of certain members of our societies such as court historians whose services bridge the gap between episodes in our historical lives. This is especially important for us as people of oral traditional culture and therefore people who lack the advantage of literal record keeping. The role of the court historians often proved to be of particular significance because important decisions affecting our societies were and still are based on oral traditional culture. That meant that records of incidents and occurrences depended largely on recall. So our historical traditions and customs relied on the memories of those people who were responsible to recall events as passed down from time immemorial. Recalling of some of these traditional customs is easier than others, especially those that are more constantly in practice, whereas others that occur less frequently can prove to be more difficult and therefore depended on the memories of court historians.

With all its shortcomings, such as memory lapses, this tradition remains one of our important social-cultural heritages. Because of their skill and in spite of their shortcomings, the court historians are often the last line of defence against usurpation of thrones, for example, or miscarriage of traditional customary justices. As the expertise of these cultures is exercised through narrative techniques, this custom and technique in communication is common practice among us as people of oral traditional culture.

Using ethnological methodology, the research has presented the various historical, social and cultural aspects of our lives including our social and liturgical rituals that we apply on occasions of libations to our ancestral spirits. The narrative approach enabled the input of relevant oral historical perspectives of our social cultures and the inclusion of materials through storytelling about some of the events about our social lives. For example, we use the narration of fables, which tell stories of legends and creatures other than human and in which we assign certain characteristics to lower creatures than ourselves that we think portray their personalities. For example, the cunning nature of the tortoise; the wisdom of the owl; the deceitful nature of the snake; the bullying nature of the leopard; the roguish nature of the fox. Our social culture places great value and significance on narrating fables, and through narration of fables we extrapolate moral precepts according to our cultural traditions and this exercise is an aspect of the ethnography of our societies.

The sources of data for this research

1   Questionnaires (pilot study)
2   Group discussions
3   Documents: Relevant articles published on topics related to the research, and 'grey literature', that is unpublished lectures and documents
4   Interviews

This research involved the use of data from sources such as interviews, documents, participant observations as in group discussions. In order to select potential participants, I had to take account of certain traditional cultural circumstances of the societies from which they the participants were to be drawn. I will briefly describe my thinking here.

The selection process of the categories of participants in the research

I considered that selecting suitable and appropriate members of our societies as candidates for interviews, group discussions, as medium for participant observation and as sources for providing documents relevant to the topic of the research would have great bearing on the outcome of the research and hence on the book.

I decided to include only people from my own social environment, as this would give me information that comes from those directly affected by the issues of the research, hence giving me an insight into how we in our societies see ourselves. I did not consider it of great interest to me to compare the views of non-members of our societies with those of the members in terms of how non-members see us. Of greater importance and relevance to me is to see how we see ourselves both at home and outside our home domains. That is:

- What were our self-perceptions and what were our representations of ourselves?
- What were our perceptions of ourselves both at home domestically, and in the international arena?
- What was our self-understanding and how did our different societies, the Igbo people in particular understand the way that we were?
- What was our self-knowledge and how do we in our different societies and different social classes see and know how we were?
- What did we know of ourselves as people; were we a nation of people or a collection of different societies of people trapped in an illusion of being members of one united country called 'Nigeria'? What was our understanding of the constitution of Nigeria regarding the societies within it?

These are the issues that I considered to be germane to my enquiry and therefore had great bearing on why I chose the groups of people to participate in the research.

For one thing these issues enter into the areas of the politics of our societies, which were hard to access partly because of physical difficulty and partly because of our mental incapacity to comprehend the political structures of the so-called united country of Nigeria. That is to say that the very nature of the colonial policies, such as application of physical force to get their way when they considered it necessary to do so as well as the psychological indoctrinations, had blunted much of the societies' sense of nationalism and patriotism. This was a psychological effect of colonialism that made it even more difficult for us to see the causes of our social ills.

In the planning of this research I have had to take into much consideration our origin and evolutions as a society of Igbo people; our characteristics, such as our celebrations of rites of passage, categories of groups of affiliations and oral cultural traditional of face-to-face interactions, which is relatively more homogeneous than literate culture.

Culture

I have had to bear in mind that we observe common customs, share common beliefs, techniques, sentiments and general outlook to life. As Emmanuel Obiechina (1975) pointed out, these characteristics have been established by ethnologists who studied West African people and the oral culture of the segmentary folk communities. That is communities like the Tiv, the Igbos, the centralised semi-urbanised societies of the Yoruba land, and the non-Islamic northern territory of the group of societies, including the aforementioned colonialists who created and named Nigeria. Ashanti in Ghana and Tellensi are the other segmentary West African societies that were studied by ethnologists and found to possess the common characteristics of oral traditional culture.

These considerations have been the key factors to guide me in my selection of suitable research participants in individual interviews, oral discussions in different group settings and in the collecting of data relevant to the research topic from different literature, including transcripts from diaries and lectures. My attempt at tape recording some of the interview processes was difficult. I had thought that this was a method that would be very appropriate for gathering data, considering the time factor. However, there was a drawback arising from such technical factors as unreliable supply of electricity. But most hindering of all was a cultural aversion to speaking into a machine and one's voice being recorded and taken away. People in this part of the world are still uncomfortable with this system of communication. It is not suggested that they would totally refuse but rather that they would not feel free and relaxed to speak. When I had asked my prospective interviewees if I could tape record my interview with them, they had not reacted favourably to that suggestion and had seemed less enthusiastic. Therefore, on balance I decided against making much use of tape recording because a freely given interview in a relaxed frame of mind would result in more reliable and more valuable data. Consequently, I relied mainly on my notes written during and after the interview (drawing on my experience as a group analyst to record as faithfully as possible the content of the interview).

The criteria that I have used for selecting participants in different methods of data collection for analysis

The criteria that I was guided by in selecting the participants were based on my assessments of the sociological factors of our societies as a people as I have discussed above.

The first of these criteria was the age generational differences among the members of our societies. Age generational differences were important in the selection of the participants. It is different from chronological age distinctions based on calendar calculations in terms of day, month and year calculations. I will clarify this further in the context of the Abiriba Igbo society.

It was not the traditional practice for every birth and death to be officially registered before the time of the colonial administration of our societies. Non-literate oral cultural societies such as ours could not and did not have systems of documentation of data such as births and deaths. Thus it was the case that births and deaths of people born before colonisation were not documented.

Consequently, any references to age that I make will be to a large extent in terms of generational age ranges or age groups of affiliations. Under this traditional method of noting people's ages, all known births within certain time periods are grouped together as belonging to the same age range and are known members of the age groups of affiliation – uke – such as lizard hunters or bird hunters, and so on as the case may be. They would identify themselves as belonging to their assigned age group as laid down by our traditions. Therefore as an example, the chronological age ranges of children belonging to the same age generational group may vary by up to four years. This has largely been the criteria for determining ages within my Abiriba Igbo society. Other societies had their formula for determining age and categories of members of their societies, such as the Yoruba people who noted the age ranges of their citizens using periods during the dynasty of their kings. So people could say they were born during the first, second or third year in the reign of king A, B, or C of their society.

Even after colonialism, when birth and deaths registrations were introduced, these were administrative practices exercised in only some selected territories such as the more urbanised capital towns and cities, especially coastal towns and cities such as Lagos, Port Harcourt, Warri, Calabar, Sapele and a number of other community settlements on river banks.

By the same token, different towns, cities and communities were classified differently as either British territories or British-protected territories in which

Figure 5.1 Members of age group of affiliation

the citizens were then categorised as British subjects or British-protected people, respectively. The responsibilities of the British colonialists for these two categories of our citizens varied according to these categorisations.

Another factor that influenced my choosing the age generational categorisation instead of chronological age categorisations was because by and large it is considered to be uncivil and disrespectful to ask people what their chronological ages were, particularly so in any case of a younger person asking such a question of an older one. Yet older age is considered to be an attribute of virtue; the older that a person is, the more virtuous that he/she is considered to be.

This meant that in practice, I had to consider chronological age factor as untenable and impractical and unreliable data available to include in the criteria to determine the categorisations of people from which to select the participants. I considered the age generational calculations as the more reliable. My knowledge of the sociology of this society, I being myself a native of it, stood me in good stead as it made it easier for me to be aware of certain factors of our lives that were important in determining some of the selection criteria that were to make the group discussions more viable and more productive.

Some of the ultimate end products of my selection criteria resulted in very few people who were old enough to be coerced into receiving the British system of education and were still alive when this research was started in 2005. Nor were there people who were actually born at the time of arrival and the beginning of colonisation of our societies in the year 1900 who were still alive in 2005. Only very few people who were born two decades after the occupation were still alive then.

The second criteria for the selection of candidates in this research was people's social class status, itself determined by two criteria. These criteria were:

1   The factor of the British system of Education and Literacy, that is those who were privileged to receive the British education and literacy and those who were not – the social class stratification system. The significance of this was that it was regarded as the quintessential credential for being recognised and accepted in our colonial and post-colonial societies.
2   The second criteria was people's social standings in their societies, the determination of this being based on the people's professional or occupational standings, such as law, medicine, nursing, engineering, ministry of religion, university lecturers and teachers, regarded as those on the higher social class category.

Traditional occupational standings such as farming, fishing and handy-crafts, such as weaving and carving were included among occupations of the lower social class standings. But natives with traditionally acclaimed high social standing, such as traditional law experts and court historians, were highly regarded too for the purpose of this research.

The significance of people's social class standing was based on the premise that people's professional and occupational standings by and large reflected the levels of their academic attainments especially in literacy and therefore their potentials for domestic and international social mobility. That is the ability to interact at home and abroad on behalf of our societies and of themselves.

So each of the generational groups consisted of:

a   The literate and well-educated category of the younger age generations of our societies.
b   The non-literate and uneducated category of the younger age generation of our societies.
c   The literate and well-educated category of the older age generation of our societies.
d   The illiterate and uneducated category of the older age generation of our societies.

Similarly among young and literate age generation, were people of low and high social standings and within the young and illiterate age generations were predominantly people of traditional occupations category such as arable farmers, fishermen, hunters and craft men and women such weavers and market traders.

The research methods employed

In particular, the ethnographic approach provided me with a useful framework: I was embarking on a journey of finding out about the social and cultural phenomena of a people's life. In other words, I was embarking on a journey of exploration which involved in essence, making, reporting and evaluating my observations on the customary behaviours in our 'Ndi Igbo' societies in particular. Conklin (1968) suggested that this is what we are concerned with in 'Ethnography'.

Because ethnography is a unique type of natural history in which the observer becomes an active participant in the observed universe, being such an intimate part of the world that is under study however, raises many questions that will be familiar to psychotherapists. Psychotherapists need to avoid falling victim to counter transference when he/she sees himself/herself in the same predicament as his/her client and is unable to maintain objectivity. It is for this reason that psychotherapists are obliged as part of their training to undergo personal or individual personal psychotherapy course of themselves as part of the requirement of their training.

As Robin Higgins (1996) again stated, the ethnographer participates overtly or covertly in people's daily lives for an extended period of time, watching what happens, listening to what is said and asking questions. However, according to Hammersley and Atkinson (1983) this raises the question of what becomes the ethnographer's own worldview, which might influence the way that they assess other people's. This presented a situation comparable with that which psychotherapists, indeed like myself, find ourselves in, occasionally. Hence the central plank of our training as psychotherapists and or group analysts is our own personal analysis which gives us the opportunity to examine and understand the genesis of some of our own behaviours and responses in our clinical working situations. Thus we are able to exercise the necessary discipline to avoid actions which may hinder our ability to carry out our clinical practices as therapists effectively.

I expected that the journey of the exploration in this ethnographic approach would take us, myself and all others involved, inwards into some hidden memories and experiences; that it might also take us outwards into the world around us, or indeed take me and my co participants in this journey into both directions one after the other or in both directions both at the same time. In other words the exploration method of the ethnographical approach, by its nature, would bring out memories of deep-seated feelings that would have lain where they were if undisturbed.

It is important to be aware of the psychological implications of the nature of the ethnographical approach given its characteristics which I have stated above. The consequences of their presence, even though they only lay dormant, might perhaps not have been related to their existence. But once the inner memories had gained expression into the external realities, they acquire a place of their own in our daily lives which we needs must respond to. Hence such exploration required a method or an approach which would be adequate for coping with the different possible outcomes as I have analysed.

In this instance the exploration involved ethnographic enquiries of the social and cultural phenomena of the life of all the societies that come under the umbrella of the colonialists' creation by the name of the country 'Nigeria'. I saw my function as that of an ethnographer with a basic task of enquiring into every aspect of the process.

In my position in the research project as that of a participant observer, I was aware of myself as a part of the group of the active participants in the ethnographic enquiry into my own natural environment as I am in reality an indigenous member of this social environment, the Igbos society. In other words, I the explorer was also the subject of the exploration; I the observer was also the subject of the observations.

I was aware of an apparent potential for counter transference reaction which might mean that I reacted to my own personal issues by losing my objectivity in the process of my observations, enquiries and conclusions.

My own personal analysis predisposed me to the advantage of being prepared for the task of the explorations and enquiries into the views, reminisces and experiences of my fellow members of our society under the colonialists' rule, with a reasonable degree of objectivity.

My enquiries included also exploring the effects of the colonial policies on all of our different traditions and cultural beliefs and our freedom to practice these traditions and customs according to the norms that govern their existence and practices. I expected the outcome of these enquiries and explorations to either vindicate or refute my basic premise that the effect of the British colonial ruling policies for all our societies under the name of Nigeria was detrimental to us the Igbo people in particular and all the other societies in general and that it was affecting our personality, the sum total of our mental make-up, as a people in our own right.

Because of all these various characteristics of the ethnographic approach to the research I considered that it would enable me to explore the various and relevant aspects of my proposition that 'the rupturing and dislocation of our cultural institutions were the consequences of the colonial policies adopted for us by the British colonial rulers of our lands'.

I felt that the ethnographic approach was appropriate in this instance because my research involved much inter-verbal communications with different people. The interactions between me and my own kin, people who were still predominately of this culture, were better suited by oral communication traditions, meaning that in effect that we had face-to-face interactions which characteristically involved observation of bodily gesticulations and facial expressions. These in their own right told their own stories of the subject matters involved. In the processes of the group discussions, for example, I found that such physical communications were often quite complementary to verbal communications even though they were unspoken and often betrayed the emotions that were attached to the verbal expressions.

Such emotions themselves might not have been revealed where only verbal expressions were used. Their detection often gave indications to a further direction of approach which elicited more information. My being a member of this social environment therefore made this approach a particularly appropriate one to use.

The questionnaire methods of collecting data

In so far as I was adopting an ethnographic approach, of undertaking a journey of finding out the social and cultural phenomena of the life of the Igbos, my people which included me, I considered the research to be both heuristic and autobiographical. Autobiographical in the sense that I, as the researcher, would be writing about myself as well as about others. I would adopt a line of enquiry that has a specific focus with the intention of making a discovery about an intended subject matter. I decided to conduct a pilot study which involved designing a questionnaire and distributing this to as many individuals and societies that I could identify as potentially being interested in the topic of my research and hence to the production of a book.

The questionnaire method of collecting data involved the structuring of questions to submit to different individuals in order to collect data which would enable me to clarify this research proposal by exploring how we were affected by colonialism and its policies.

The process involved a form of dialogue between myself and the research participant from whom I was collecting data. It is important in this exercise to avoid leading the respondent into the answer to a question but rather to enable him/her to give spontaneous response to the questions. It may be necessary to add a supplementary question that would help to test the authenticity of the answer given to the main question.

According to Clark Moustakas (1990), such dialogue should not be ruled by the clock but by inner experiential time, as he put it. In the dialogue that takes place between the two, it is proper to encourage situations that allow ideas, thoughts, feelings and images to unfold and be expressed naturally. Rogers (1969) in his essay 'Toward a science of the Person' suggested that the quest is complete when one has an opportunity to tell one's story to a point of natural closing.

An auto-ethnographic context

My aim in seeking to discover and the task of achieving that discovery, demanded of me a passionate desire to know, a devotion and commitment to pursue a question that is strongly connected to my own identity and selfhood as a member of my society.

Indeed, I have stated that I saw the task that confronted me here as one in which I embarked on a journey of exploration which would take me and all the other participants involved into different areas of our memories including hidden memories and experiences in the effort to discover a fundamental truth about ourselves, myself at least as natives of our societies.

Indeed, Moustakas stated that the awakening of such a question (question such as that which would lead to the discovery) comes through an inward clearing and an intentional readiness and determination to discover the fundamental truth regarding the meaning and essence of one's own experience and that of others.

Given that one of the essential characteristic of the enquiry is the use of questions to discover the social and cultural phenomena of a people like us, it became necessary for me to ensure first and foremost that I was clearly in touch with my own passionate feelings about the subject that I set out to explore. That meant making clear in my own mind that I had a question of my own which was compelling enough to serve me as a path that will as Polanyi (1969) put it, 'sustain curiosity, involvement and participation with full energy and resourcefulness over a lengthy period of time'.

Recruitment of participants

Having considered people that I felt would be suitable to participate in the research, I was confronted next by the issues of where and how to reach them. This issue applied just as much with my locating prospective participants in the

United Kingdom where I was resident, as it did with other places as far afield as the United States of America and Europe and our home societies. There was also an added issue of how to encourage the people and gain their trust so that they would cooperate with me in my project.

I knew that certain factors such social conditions of those living in their second homes such as the United Kingdom, the United States of America and Europe, would affect their decisions on whether to cooperate with me on my project or not. This particular issue refers to the political status of some West Africans who are living abroad for various reasons, being perhaps refugee status or illegal immigrants. They regard any involvement in something which could expose their presence in the country of their domicile as a risk that they cannot take. They would therefore not feel free to participate in projects that risk their true identities being revealed. It becomes an issue of long process of persuading and reassuring that confidentiality and anonymity would be observed. This had an impact on the length of time that they took to decide on what to do about my request. The geographical distances between me in the United Kingdom and the United States of America, and Europe, was also an important factor regarding the length of time that it took people's responses to reach me.

I had decided to limit the participant in this research to only the natives of the autonomous societies that are grouped under the name of the country of 'Nigeria'. My acting on that decision brought to light the realities of the differences that existed among these societies. These differences were also reflected in the attitudes of the different respondents first to the idea of my conducting this research programme and in particular to the specific subject of the research. This was evident in the distribution of the number of people that responded from our different societies as far as I was able to determine people's respective societies of origin.

In the final analysis then, I was faced with the following issues:

1. Locating the prospective participants
2. Reaching them
3. Developing an agreement of time and place and means of meeting where applicable
4. Considering the best ways of creating an atmosphere or climate that would encourage trust, openness and self-disclosure among us.

As I pointed out earlier, these were common difficulties that I had to deal with irrespective of where the prospective participants were to be located.

To deal with the issues that I have enumerated here, I proceeded with sampling; by approaching people in different organisations of members of as many of our different societies as I could. I briefed them on what I was planning to do and how they could help me with doing it. I enlisted the help of people who knew different bodies and organisations which was particularly helpful to me in making contacts with these potential candidates.

Ultimately there were a total of 585 participants available for me select from to participate in the different methods of data collection for the research.

The questionnaire processes

The categorisations discussed above shows that the selections of the participants in the questionnaire responses were based to a large extent on the sociological factors of our societies, particularly those of the members of my Igbo societies.

I was able to compile lists of names of individuals as well as lists of names of organisations and I was then able to contact the individuals within the organisations as well as contact individuals outside as was applicable, with the questionnaires. My thinking behind this approach was to save time and also to minimise the chances of people replying to make excuses about why they might not be able to participate in the project. I was concerned that people's fantasies about the contents of the questionnaire could deter them from cooperating with me in the research. However, I assured them that they were under no obligation to participate in the project, and should feel under no duress to participate in it, but that I would very much appreciate their cooperation by taking part in it.

I dispatched my prepared questionnaires to individuals and to groups respectively. In effect, I allowed people less opportunity to consider saying yes or no to participating in the research. In the cases of groups I adopted two approaches: I addressed the questionnaires to the individual members as contained in the lists that were sent to me with the consents of the willing members. In such cases, I enclosed stamped self-addressed envelopes for their replies assuring each person or group as applicable of the confidentiality of the information that they would provide me with. I am aware that in a sense I presumed to have their informal consent to participate in this research bearing in mind that they might not respond to the questionnaire. That was a risk that existed even with people who had said that they would respond to the questionnaires.

I gave everyone in the groups and individual participants the assurances also that any information that they gave me would be used solely for academic studies. These assurances were given in all the cases, in order to reassure participants, and to develop rapport with each and every one as much as that was possible and then go on to establishing agreement of times to meet, places to meet and means of communicating as was necessary.

With the consent of the organisation as a whole and their members individually I sent to the organisations bulk packages of the questionnaires enclosing self-addressed stamped envelopes to distribute to their members. I followed up some people by telephone in the evenings when my particular telephone tariff contract allowed me to make calls free of charge to people who lived within certain geographical distances in the United Kingdom. I enlisted the help of some people who knew me as well as some members of some of the organisations, as well as knew individuals that they thought were potentially suitable to participate in the research. I followed these up and after satisfying myself that they were suitable, I elected to include them. In the cases of some of the participants in the distant and faraway places, my helpful friends spoke on my behalf at the initial time to assure groups and organisations of my honesty and integrity.

The results of all these efforts varied widely; some organisations were less forthcoming with their responses to my request and as a result I received fewer responses from them. It was never made clear to me why those who did not respond failed to do so. One could only assume that this was either due to their having misplaced their questionnaires, or due to procrastination arising from their attaching little importance to the research. In such cases I simply sent off other copies of the questionnaires to the people that I felt needed to be prompted and with notes asking them to accept my apology for seeming to be impatient. This yielded the desired effects as many more completed questionnaires were returned. Some of the responses were done in the form of essays using the different items in the questionnaire as headings for the different points that they were making. This approach had some merit as it gave the respondents wider scope to include points that the structure of my questionnaires had not anticipated. Ultimately, I had enough willing respondents to respond to the questionnaires.

I estimated that most of the participants in this methods of data collection were people born between 1970 and 1985 and their ages therefore ranged from between 30 years to 25 years. There were about 200 of these available to participate in the research.

As an example of one of the questionnaires and a response:

Q: 'When and how did you become conscious of colonialism in Nigeria?'
A: 'When I was in secondary school via history of Nigeria lessons.'
Q: 'What did you understand it to mean?'
A: 'The rule of a country by another.'
Q: 'How did it affect you as a member of your society, e.g as a native of the Abiriba or any other of the territories that come under the name 'Nigeria' from which you come?'
A: 'I wasn't affected, it does not affect me.'
Q: 'Did it affect your religion, your traditional education in the customs and practices of your society of the Igboland?'
A: 'I am not aware of having had any other religion, so I have no basis for comparison. Similarly, I have no idea of traditional system of education.'
Q: 'It may be helpful to consider the impact of the British system of education on yourself and your social environment.'
A: 'I consider the impact to be positive, it has had the effect of equipping me with ideas and skills for running my own affairs, and contributing to the members of my social environment.'
Q: 'How did you come to be educated?'
A: 'By going to formal school, the Missionary school.'

Q: 'How has this affected your life?'
A: 'I am able to relate with people from different social and religious backgrounds, and improved the quality of my life. It has enabled me to have well informed discussions about life.'

Once I had read through all the responses and noted the different themes arising, I began to plan for organising group discussions.

The processes of collection of data for the research through the method of group discussions including the process of selection of the participants in the groups and my role as a participant observer in the groups

From the onset I had decided to use participant observation because by creating an appropriate space the group leader makes it possible for the participants to recreate lived experiences.

Group participators have at their disposal a variety of means such as narrative descriptions, dialogues and other materials of personal nature to recall past experiences which can be painful as well as pleasant. The emphasis was on reproducing and recreating personal experiences in the here and now and relating them to the present realities. These potentials for the use of a group situation made it possible to realise the aims of the ethnographic processes of fully exploring the customary behaviour of our societies by observing and evaluating my observations. As a participant observer I was as equally involved as any other member of the group in the processes of finding out about our customary ways of life while at the same time, I was observing the processes as they developed.

The processes for the selection of the participants for group discussions

The group sessions consisted of people who were estimated to have been born between 1925 and 1945 and who were therefore estimated to be aged between about 80 years to 60 years with the total number of participants from this group estimated as about 135.

A significant factor which needs to be mentioned about the process that I followed in the selection was that it was biased in the sense that I had preference for Abiriba Igbos. Following the categorisations of participants into age generational groups and social standings, all those selected for group meetings were Abiriba Igbos in the category of the older age generations of both the educated and literate and the non-educated and illiterate.

The Abiriba Igbos also represented for me a source of a more easily accessible sample of interviewees because they were the people with whom I shared and still share the same social cultures in the same social environment of our Igbo society. I expected to share stronger and more meaningful evidence of the effect of the colonial policy on us and would therefore feel in a stronger position to draw conclusions on their effects. I would be in position to ask myself such questions as why did I feel this way about this or that situation, whereas, this or that member of our society felt differently about the same situation and we were all in the same situation at the same time?

Secondly, other members of our societies who would also had qualified in this category but were illiterate in the English language and belonged to other societies of our geographical territories spoke different vernacular languages from mine. I was therefore handicapped by the language factor from communicating with them. My attempts to reach some of the educated and literate members of this category but who were from other societies and cultural groups within our geographical territories proved to be impractical. It involved working through different people from the different societies. It was to be a very difficult endeavour particularly because of the vast geographical area that it involved and given the very poor communications system, very unreliable transport system and almost non-existent data base of information available to rely upon.

I was however more successful in obtaining data from this category of participants through their response to my questionnaires. One of the advantages of the mass education in the English language had been that those who had received English literacy education were able to communicate with one another in the in English. Using English also made it possible for a second lingua franca in the form of pidgin English to evolve. This enabled many more people from different societies of our territories to communicate with one another. But the use of pidgin English is limited in its scope because, it is mainly spoken and not written. It is not a common practice to write letters and make documents using pidgin English in interpersonal communications. It is limited in its scope also by the fact that it has the characteristic of a dialect, in that like dialects, pidgin English spoken in particular areas tends to be peculiar to the area since they evolve from the mixture of the English language and the local language or dialect.

In this circumstance that I was in, I had a group of Abiriba Igbos in the Older age generation category within the age ranges of between 65 and 80. Although they were fewer in number than the participants of the younger age groups, they represented people who were just old enough to have experienced life during and after the colonial regime in our societies, as I myself had.

The members of this group themselves indicated that they preferred to have an oral face-to-face group discussion on the subject matter with me rather than participate in the research by any other method.

Because of their preference for face-to-face interactions, characteristic of our people, members who qualified for selection for this group, also qualified for selection to provide data through their responses to interviews.

Even the literate ones in this group preferred the oral, free floating and free associational discussions in the group on the subject. Lack of literacy of some of the members of this group was no hindrance to either myself, or to the others in the group, because we all shared a common language – 'Igbo' – and we were even more comfortable conducting our discussions in the Igbo language. In fact both the group discussions and the interviews with members selected from this group were conducted mainly in our native language, Igbo. This category of participants numbered about 135 in all who were available from which to select participants for group sessions and for interview sessions. The difference between those from this group who participated in group discussions and those who opted for interview was made mainly through time constraints. Within this group, the social and economic circumstances of the prospective participants were important factors which militated against some of them more than the others. Even at such a great age, some of these participants were still obliged to go out to pursue some occupation or the other, to eke out some living and therefore were not always available when the others were. We made the most economic use of our available time, as for example, when there were not enough participants available for a group session.

I searched out individuals of this group who were available and arranged to hold interviews with as many of them as possible, given the time that was available and following my already drawn out questions. As I stated earlier, time was an important factor since I was obliged to travel to my Igboland to conduct the groups with these particular participants as well as conduct interviews.

The participant members of this group, both in the group and in the interview sessions, felt very much at home in their situation because of our common heritage of language custom and social environment.

The group sessions

My own first-hand knowledge of our cultural traditions was a great advantage in helping me to create a suitable space and atmosphere for the group participants to speak freely about their experiences and to reminisce. I realised that I had to guard against making auto-suggestions especially given the likelihood that I would relate to other people's experiences.

The method that I adopted in conducting this group was peculiar to the special need for which the groups were convened. The groups were unlike therapeutic groups which I had conducted with the purpose of providing psychotherapy to the participants. Members of such groups are encouraged to exercise freedom of purpose, and are not usually set any agenda other than the aim of exploring feelings as a means of discovering alternatives to undesirable tendencies. For this special group I set an agenda for all the participants which was to share feelings arising from their experiences of life with the British colonisers of our lands during the period in history between 1900 to 1960.

The processes of the group meeting were that following our traditions and customs I welcomed my interviewees by presenting them with white chalk dug from the earth and encrusted in a groove at one end of a carved wooden ornament. This is for us a sign of peace and welcome from the host, myself, as the head of my household to my guests. They are obliged by tradition, duty and honour to rub their fingers in the chalk and mark their wrist with it to reciprocate the gesture of the good will that I had extended to them as their host.

This ritual is followed with another of offering of kola nuts of the four cotyledon variety called 'Orji Igbo' – Igbo kola nut – in another carved wooden container and also with a groove in the centre of it for hot pepper sauce to dip the kola nut in and eat. I would then offer my guests some drink, native palm wine or any of the imported alcohol drinks according to their preferences.

We all share these after the customary ritual libation to thank God almighty for his blessings on us and on our ancestors.

It was customary for me to share these welcoming presents with my guests as standard procedures in our Abiriba Igbo customs and traditions and I have always been proud and ready to carry out these traditions. Therefore the occasions of these group discussions with my fellow members of the older generations of our society were never an exception.

On completion of these traditional formalities, I introduced the topic of the group meeting in the manner that I have outlined earlier. That is that I had asked them to come and share with me as fellow citizens of our society their memories of the colonial era. What were their experiences and their feelings then and now? What did they think of the state of our society then and what do they think of it now? How did they feel that their lives had been affected if at all? How were their lives affected? Did they think that our society was affected by the system of the colonial rule over us? These were questions that I put to them at different times at my different meetings with each group when we met.

I had always known by experience that requests for these kind of meetings received the best response from our people if they were made to feel that they were well regarded as wise elder members of our society, because we value dearly our respect for one another, our dignity and our honour for ourselves and for one another.

We always aspire to make efforts over the years of our social and ego developmental lives, to lay foundations for behaviours that would bear fruits that would nourish and benefit our society as a whole and our spiritual lives as a people. Also which would yield the fruits of morality, communalism and sustained sense of nationalism. As the groups consisted of a good number of participants of my own age group, I was able through my approach towards them to project and create a relaxed atmosphere which enabled them to assume and maintain their composure and cultural dignity. They felt free to express their deep feelings about their present and their past lives and times in our society during the period of the foreign occupation and afterwards. Some of the group members occasionally seemed to be seeking reassurance from me or expecting me to concur with what they were saying by adding words or sentences such as, 'you know about these things, how they occurred, you were there too'.

In order to ensure objectivity I found it safer to avoid completing sentences when, following the manner of the conversation, a speaker would leave gap in the flow of his sentences by stopping speaking in mid-sentence as he is filled with emotion brought up by recalled memory of some past experience. In spite of the fact that such memories were painful and unpleasant, they were evidence that the participant felt safe enough in the group and with the group to allow himself to show such emotion. For we are proud people. So for example, at such times someone would express such sentiment as 'you were there, you remember how it was too; the problem that people under went for not paying their taxes in time'. At such juncture in the group interactions, at such level of intimacy, there was a risk of being left to carry on, as it were by completing the sentence and filling in the gap with my own words or sentences.

This had the risk of leading me to using my own word or words which might have been different from those that the group member might have chosen even if his actual chosen word or words were synonymous with mine. I judged that if I did take the bait, as it were, we would never have known the words that the group member would have used. Yet our words indicate what we feel emotionally and internally. Even when we disguise our words they still have some emotional value which psychology can assist us to access. It was important therefore for me in my other role, that is as a participant observer to bear this in mind and not to allow my role as a participant to militate against my role as an observer too.

The group participants sometimes said how they had suddenly 'felt transported into those days as I speak', recalling memories in feeling of the sorrow that they felt at times past during the rule of the colonialists, but which had been brought on here and now by the mental journey back into the past during the rule of 'Nde Beke' – White people.

Most members remembered the sad lament which we all sang to reflect our sorrow during the times of our oppressions in the hands of the colonialists saying: 'Ma obughu Nwa Beke, Igbo anyi mara ihe anyi geme' – If it were not for the White men with their oppressive might, we the Igbos know what we can do.

The words of this lamentation in actual fact make statements about the way that the colonial oppressions prevented us from acting freely by taking necessary actions to defend ourselves against our oppressors when we had felt oppressed. In some instances these oppressions took the form of military force using our very own fellow natives under the military command of the British colonising officers of course.

Reference list

Conklin, H.C. (1968) 'Ethnography', in *International Encyclopaedia of Social Science*. Vol. 5. New York: Macmillan & Free Press, pp. 172–178.

Hammersley, M. and Atkinson, P. (1983) *Ethnography: Principles in Practice*. London: Tavistock Publications.

Higgins, R. (1996) *Approaches to Research: A Handbook for Those Writing a Dissertation.* London: Jessica Kingsley Publishers, p. 22.

Moustakas, C. (1990) *Heuristic Research: Design, Methodology and Applications.* Newbury Park: Sage Publications, Inc.

Obiechina, E. (1975) *Culture, Tradition and Society in the West African Novel.* African Studies Series 14. Cambridge: Cambridge University Press.

Polanyi, M. (1969) *Knowing and Being: Essays by Michael Polanyi.* Edited by M Grene. Chicago: University of Chicago Press.

Rogers, C.R. (1969) 'Towards a science of the person', in A.J. Sutich and M.A. Vich eds., *Readings in Humanistic Psychology.* New York: Macmillan.

Chapter 6

Analysis of and reflections on the group discussions

When I started to prepare for working on this book, it was from the perspective that the main outcome of the colonial ruling policies was in the dislocations and ruptures of our Igbo cultural traditions and social institutions, with detrimental consequences to our way of life and our integrity as a people. As a group analytic psychotherapist, I wanted to reflect on how group analysis might be applied to those who had gone through the trauma of colonial oppression, like ourselves as West Africans. I wanted to explore these perspectives and to know more about the way others from my society experienced the impact of British colonialism. The questionnaire responses from the pilot study had given me a sense of important questions that might be put to those people who agreed to participate in group and individual interviews. I have discussed the criteria I used to bring people together, and how I saw my role. There is no doubt that the material from these live experiences demonstrates how powerful the impact of colonialism was and still is on the various generations, whether they are still living in 'Nigeria' or elsewhere. I have reflected on some of the main issues that came up.

Understanding of colonialism

Among my peers, perspectives on colonialism not surprisingly differed with some holding very positive views and others extremely negative, according to their own experiences. The following quotes, taken from the questionnaires, illustrate this:

> Colonialism has never affected me as an individual holding my own or living my life in the society. Seemingly, the rites which obtain in our society and are so admirable in themselves are not in essence prescriptive. If one performs one or the other, one becomes entitled to the dignity attached to it.

And:

> I am not conscious of any effect that colonialism had on me as a citizen of a colonial territory. If there were inadequacy in the provision of medical facilities, construction of good roads etc., I cannot remember attributing it to colonialism then or now.

The internal conflict in our societies between 1966 and 1970 claimed the lives of a substantial number of people from the different societies and social groups that make up 'Nigeria'. Tribal mistrust deepened among members and betrayed to a large extent the illusion of the existence of a united country. Some participants from the groups referred to that conflict and to the younger men who were embroiled in it as they became disillusioned with the system of governing this so-called united country. They expressed such sentiments as: 'we did not have things like this when White men were ruling us'.

Given that these participants included those who were not yet born when the White men ruled us, one could only infer that these sentiments arose from the version of the colonial ruling policies that they were taught in history lessons in school, about the British Empire and their colonies. Fear of our native military rulers and suspicions about their probity heightened as allegations were made of their exploitations of our natural resources, just as their predecessors had done. Our own native citizens continued where the colonial rulers before them left off, in the practice of exploitation.

These participants who were born post the colonial era, were in effect largely re-enforcing and re-emphasising their belief that the British colonialists' values were better than our native ones. To any degree that this was true, it was not because we could not govern ourselves but rather that the resources to enable us to do so had been sabotaged by the colonialists through the mechanism of the dislocations and rupturing of the structures of our cultural traditions and cultural institutions. Yet they asked us to build our societies with resources that were ill-suited to our purpose and to our own ways of life. Such systems were suited for dominating people and not for guiding them to everyone's benefit. Given 'freewill' and human rights, we might have taken different routes more suited to our culture and traditions and our destiny would have been shaped by us with different consequences. We would have been guided by sets of circumstances more in accordance with our traditional beliefs.

As continuing observation on the outcome of responses from this category of participants, I would comment that they did not, and could not, have a basis for comparing experiences of living in the two regimes of our colonised societies and our societies under the governance of our own native citizens.

There were of course material colonial legacies, such as recreational clubs, ballroom dancing clubs, tennis, swimming clubs, schools and churches all providing the background for 'delusions of grandeur'. With only the history of these material relics to rely on it was difficult for the respondents of this age generational category to do more than empathise with the frustrations of the older age members, such as myself, the author, who also experienced first-hand the consequences of the colonial policies on our society.

I believe these were important responses which had significant bearing on what this age generational category of participants brought to the research, both in their questionnaire responses of the pilot study and in the interviews.

It is clear, then, that there were different experiences as lived by the different age generations over the periods of pre-colonialism, the period of colonialism and post-colonialism when we were handed the reigns of self-governance.

I personally related to the experiences expressed by some of the members in these discussions. For example, the views that exposure to other world cultures leaves its imprint on those so exposed yet total abandonment of our own traditional culture in favour of the alien cultures would leave us at the margin of any claims to having an identity as a people. We would only be subordinates without independent characteristics thus bereft of any cultural or personal identity of our own. We would have no basis for claiming to be a people and entitled to resisting against being treated otherwise.

In the group discussions we shared common experiences of emotions of anger and frustration at the outcome of our recalled memories of the colonial abuses that we received. But these arose from the different circumstances of our lives in our society; for instance, in my own particular case, my anger and frustration arose from my recalling being a member of a Christian family and how this culminated in a great anxiety-provoking situation for me when it seemed that my life as a Christian was threatening to deny me my right to celebrate one of my traditional rites of passage (see Vignette 1.1).

Education

As I have said, the British education system brought its benefits, not least in requiring that we learn the English language. It also enabled communication between societies which had many different languages. As one participant said:

> The British produced an effective educational system to which the Nigerian independence may be proudly attributed to when it came in October 1960. It was that system of education which became an eye opener to the exploitation and malevolence of colonialism.

The same participant continued:

> The educational system it bequeathed to Nigeria was unimpeachable from Primary to Secondary, and finally to university level when the University of Ibadan became functional in 1949.
>
> It must be said with commendation that the missionaries played a vital role in the educational system in Nigeria. It was that system which created a formidable cadre of Nigerian elite who later became the vanguard of Nigerian independence.

Yet, this participant added:

> It may be said that the summer of independence had left behind a winter of gloom. This is not an indictment against independence but on a failure of leadership, exacerbated by the misfortune which betook the country after independence. Corruption blooms as a thriving major industry while the 'giant of Africa' struggles painfully for a role. It was not what the cessation of British colonial occupation of Nigeria was meant to be.

Religion

Religion is an aspect of Nigerian social life that provokes divergent views, namely about how it was affected by colonial ruling policies. Opinions were divided about the effects of the colonialists' attitudes towards our traditional religious practices. The older generation in the groups expressed the most dissatisfaction with the approach of the colonialists. This was principally because of the strong link between our traditional religious beliefs with all our other social institutions, as our religious beliefs form the basis of these institutions. The denigration of our religion coupled with restricted access to practice then threatened to turn our pious nature to one of apostasy. The methods adopted by the colonial missionaries to convert us into the Christian religion were by and large forceful and coercive. The trauma that we experienced during the advent of the introduction of Christianity and the manner in which it was imposed on us continues to bring back echoes of doom to each of the members of the groups.

However, some participants were relaxed about the changes:

> I do not think that the colonial rule was or has been the bane of our folklore or traditional practices. Some traditional practices may lapse into desuetude because people's attitude had changed. This is particularly so where such practices are not enforceable.

And:

> Pressure on land because of population will continue to affect some of the traditional practices. Sons and daughters have no inhibition how to organise their marriages. Our travels and trade abroad have affected our outlook on life and possibly our values, and will so continue.

And:

> I am relaxed and unaffected by how much a celebrant of Igwa Mang or any other ceremony spends in excess to achieve uniqueness or to make it a particular occasion for the people.

To my question. 'Did colonialism affect your religion?' the response was:

> I had no other religion, so no basis for comparison. Similarly no idea of traditional education.

This participant felt that the impact of education under colonialism had been entirely positive on his life in helping to relate to people from other social and religious backgrounds.

Another, older, participant took a balanced view of colonialism:

> Like many things in life, colonialism in Nigeria had its bright and gloomy sides. On the brighter side, it brought together various tribes and people with their varying cultures and languages and formed the country called Nigeria, albeit for the sinister interest of the colonialists. Nevertheless, it brightened the horizon for the unity we are still seeking. Colonialism brought western education and culture; western-style developments which included hospitals, roads and railway services. These formed invaluable bridges for fostering understanding and unity among a people who would otherwise be alien and hostile to each other. Western religious practices must not be forgotten for their huge influences which brought sobering good effects to areas formerly pervaded by heartless inhuman practices.

However, as this participant continued:

> For all that can be said in favour of colonialism it still had many gloomy sides. It was exploitative and it impoverished its subjects. It scorned the people's indigenous languages, traditions and cultures thereby giving them little or no attention in schools. Its educational system was geared to the colonialists' tradition and culture . . . traditional medicines and herbs were seen to be the embodiment of evils. On the whole, colonialism viewed native institutions and customs with suspicion and hence set about to discourage their growth.

Many members volunteered information that they had often been made to wonder why the God of justice, the God that bears witness to the innocent had left the 'Bekes' (White people) to go unpunished for their sin of desecrating the shrines of our ancestors. Some still say today, though I do not believe with much conviction, that the White men will yet reap the whirlwind for their acts of sacrilege in our societies:

As one participant said:

> The view of any right-thinking Abiriba indigene should be to uphold tradition and support vehemently the celebration of all our age-honoured heritages. Other countries and people all over the world show pride in

their traditions and national heritages and are identified by them. Abiriba should be no exception. Our customs and heritages are our identity locally and abroad. There is no fetish about Igwa Mang and it is malicious and hypocritical to link it to fetishness or local politics. There is need that all sides should unite and in the end 'give Caesar that which is his'. Let better sense prevail.

Perhaps one sustaining factor that maintains the beliefs of this age generational category of participants is yet our religion, their strong and continued belief, because in spite of all the efforts of the colonial missionaries they did not succeed in converting as many natives as they tried to into Christianity. Even those who were converted maintained elements of our traditional religious beliefs entrenched in their psyche, as that which made them who they were and who they largely remain as a people. This dimension of the colonial ruling policies was a very strong factor in hardening the attitudes of this age generational category of participants. They demonstrated this by their very strong resentment against colonialism and its legacies left to their generation and even later generations; and by their more proactive participations in our various traditional religious rites while at the same time not yielding to pressures to conform to Christian religious traditions.

Significant among the outcomes of the group discussions is that they demonstrated how varied the experiences of the effects of the colonial policies are. Amid the expressed experiences of the younger age generational category as the uncritical acceptance of everything British as superior to everything of our own traditional societies, there are other views among them that acknowledge the existence of adverse consequences of colonial ruling policies. But the well-educated and high social standing members of the older age generational category lamented most about what our societies had lost through the policies of the colonial regime. They highlighted the fact that although we had the benefit of literacy, which stands us in good stead particularly at an international level, it sadly ill-equipped us for domestic harmony.

Summary

The outcome of the discussions and interviews and testimonies from different people in the different categories showed that no category maintained only one attitude or point of view about the consequences of the colonial policies on our societies.

The responses in each category showed the variability of feelings about being colonised and attitudes towards the colonisers. These variations reflected the age generational variations also. Nevertheless, each category found something about the legacies of the colonial ruling policies that they could count as a legitimate basis for crediting their claim to our being a 'burden to the White man'. By the same token, even the younger age group who seemed to see nothing but virtues in the White men's ruling policies, conceded that the White men did some wrong things against us. These were the views of those people who were born after the end of active colonisation and whose main source of awareness of what colonialism meant was in the lessons they received in classrooms on the history of the British Empire, telling them how things came to be as they were in our societies. Our own students of history and the British Constitution could only experience the legacies bequeathed to us by the colonial policies but could not experience the policies in practice, whereby they could have judged through direct and personal experience of them in action.

Here was an example of the differences in the knowledge of what happened to us and with us during the period of the colonialists' occupation of our society. Those who were not present at the time could not know what happened. They only have history to fill the gaps left in their knowledge – and most of the history was about the British Empire, written by the British as they wanted it to be known. This situation left us with a legacy of divided virtues of those who had direct experience of colonialism and those who only had a theory of what had happened, or what colonialism was through history lessons about the British Empire and its colonies.

This category of participants had a large number of literate persons among them who were educated in the British system at home and overseas in the English speaking countries, principally Britain and the United States of America. They learned about colonialism from teachings by British teachers and from text books written by British academics. However, their education did not include the teaching of the history of our native and traditional ways of life, and the ways that they were before the colonialists destroyed them, having relegated them to the category of 'primitive culture'.

So the understanding of colonialism by the younger category of participants was the colonialists' version of it, the hallmark of which was the proverbial claim of suffering the 'White man's burden' of having to civilise the primitive culture of the Black man at great pains to themselves.

A good number of the respondents in this category had, in fact, answered one of my pilot questionnaire questions, 'What do you understand colonialism to be?' with similar responses, such as, 'I understood colonialism to be foreign rule and foreign subjugation', adding, 'Today I understand it to be almost normal pattern of human historical interactions. Stronger nations will always find reasons and excuses to attack, invade and subjugate weaker nations, mostly for economic reasons'.

Although not using exactly the same words, many expressed the same sentiments. They emphasised their belief that 'nowadays no-one can reasonably succeed in life or make an appreciable impact on his age or his society without the benefit of a good education'.

The emphasis was obviously on the British system of education as our native system was largely considered to be primitive and therefore not capable of helping the educated to 'succeed' in life through the qualities I have stated here.

A further outcome of the responses from this category was an overall view that what may be seen as the ills of colonial policies for our societies and by some members of that society were not the only culprit in the inventory of the problems that we experienced from the colonial policies. They felt that these ills should be seen in the context of cultural relativity: that is, in the sense that all cultures and dynamics of societies are functions of various interacting social forces, including those of other and different cultures in different societies. In other words, our societies would at some point or other come into contact with other races and cultures who would have influenced our direction of development. Therefore they argued that the detrimental effects of the colonial policies may have been exaggerated.

I accept this as a sociological fact, and that there might be other factors at play in bringing about the social conditions that obtained in our societies during and after the time of colonialism. This situation has, however, a corollary which is that the effects of different sets of social circumstances on our societies would have been judged according to their merits and demerits to our welfare. More importantly, whatever are the sets of circumstances that culminate in the condition that a people find themselves in, the people are nevertheless obliged to understand what forces have brought them to where they are. They need that understanding in order to know why things are as they are and therefore what to avoid if they want change, and what to continue with if they want to maintain the status quo.

Some of the participants added yet a different reaction to the effects of colonialism such as their understanding of colonial policy to be a policy of the 'imposition of the will of one people or nation over another and the forceful governance of their subjects'. They interpreted what they so understood as being the consequence of the slavery mentality of the White man which continues to dominate their reasoning about themselves as superior beings to the black-skinned man. The stereotype idea of the colour 'black' being inferior to the colour 'white' reigns supreme yet in the minds of these participants. In their own way, these participants expressed their resentments to the colonialists' unilateral actions to create an illusory united country which they named 'Nigeria' from a large number of different, independent and autonomous states who had their distinct cultures and social traditions. They argued that this unilateral political action of the colonisers eclipsed the identities of all the autonomous societies which were included as being part of the illusory one, 'Nigeria'. Thereby they stripped these societies of their pride, dignity and identity as a people.

The total number of participants in the research from this group was estimated to be 250 and they were people born between 1945 to 1950 and in the final analysis, despite attempts to present a balanced perspective, they gave the view that colonialism brought to our societies more ills than benefits.

To conclude, in the words of one of the participants:

Today post-colonial Nigeria has sadly remained under the clutches of a new kind of colonialism – neo-colonialism and sadly been replayed albeit by our own leaders who are no better than the imperialists themselves.

What we have witnessed is a big failure of the leadership to carry along its citizens. It has therefore left an endless void, civil strife, corruption and an inability for the country to move forward in a progressive way that its citizenry will be proud of. Tribalism, nepotism, mediocrity, military coup d'état are all common features of our political life.

I identify with some others in our societies today who believe that this state of affairs culminated in the military force coming into the scene in the governance of our societies as we witnessed in the January 15th 1966 coup d'état. The seeds of colonialism are, in my view, still festering.

Chapter 7

Two cultures, one identity

Reflections on my attempts to bring together experiences from two conflicting cultures during my attempt to become an intercultural group psychotherapist

In this chapter, I aim to explore how the insights I have gained from my research could contribute to the theory and practice of group psychotherapy, both in the UK and elsewhere. I aim to make an original contribution to the construction of a theory that is culturally sensitive and able to be applied when working as a therapist with non-Europeans and other cultural groups who may be considered to fall under the political economic category of ethnic minorities. These would include people from West African cultural origin.

Having experienced trainings and clinical practices in analytic psychotherapy and in group analytic psychotherapy, and with the findings from my research, I have re-examined the place of Western models of psychotherapy as a treatment option for people of non-European ethnic minority groups. I would argue that this is a relevant enquiry since non-European members of the ethnic minority groups in the United Kingdom are being offered psychotherapy treatments with, in my experience (as a long-term practising group psychotherapist and supervisor and member of my Church), very little success. Moreover many that I have encountered have great reservations and even suspicion about the suitability of psychotherapy as a treatment option.

It is my belief, based on many years of experience working as a psychotherapist and within NHS mental health services, that the reason for the apparent lack of success with psychotherapy treatments for West African and Afro-Caribbean clients may be because they had been referred without clear understanding by the referrers of the crucially important factor of their cultural heritage and without due regard to the causes of the social problems that they feel indicate psychotherapy as a treatment option. Such problems cannot be generalised in the same way as those of physical illnesses which in the main are problems of human biology and physiology although there may also be contributing social factors (e.g., obesity, smoking, stress and so on).

The problems for which psychotherapy is indicated often arise from dysfunctions of social norms and conventions which often begin with problems in the family, problems of the social order of the society of which the person requiring treatment is a member. That is of conforming with or deviating from the norms by which the society is governed and boundaries maintained to ensure feelings of security within one's social network. Therefore in all situations in which psychotherapy is indicated as an appropriate treatment for a social problem, the most important factor to be considered is the social norms by which the society governs itself and maintains order and boundaries of ethics and morality.

This fact has been recognised by many who have been concerned with what is the appropriate model of psychotherapy for those who need it. Oyewole, writing in Punch Online, November 2013, about Nigerian attitudes to mental health, commented that:

> Africans perceive ill health to have material, moral, supernatural and prenatural causes which can only be determined by physical intervention and divination. Exclusive research efforts have shown that Africans generally believe that disruptive behaviour and breaking of taboos are punishable through misfortunes and mental illness.

Osuji (2006) in his paper, 'The purpose of Psychotherapy, secular and spiritual' pointed out that: 'Africans, as a whole, do not go to professional psychotherapists for help with their psychological issues. They tend to consult significant others, such as parents, uncles, aunts etc for help'. He suggests that:

> white psychotherapists, generally, do not know how to communicate with African Americans and too readily give them serious diagnoses, justifying medicinal intervention.... Clearly Africans and African Americans have to learn to express their issues in words that therapists can understand, so that they could be helped through talk based psychotherapy rather than have their bodies pumped full of destructive medications.

These authors lay emphasis on constructing models which recognise the people's social-cultural traditions, their belief systems, cultural practices and moral codes of conduct. Part of the function of maintaining the boundaries of behaviours for the survival and safety of the society is to exclude from the sociocultural norms all anomic behaviours. Gordon C. Nagayama Hall (2001) embraced this issue by recognising socio-cultural contexts as a paramount factor in constructing an appropriate model of psychotherapy and it was because of Inga-Britt Krause's awareness of the importance of cross-cultural factors in any process of psychotherapy practice that she drew the attention of psychotherapists, psychoanalysts and counsellors to the likely pitfalls in cross-cultural communications (1998, 2014).

Hall wrote about empirical, ethical and conceptual issues in psychotherapy research with ethnic minorities and argued that there is an increasing demand for psychotherapy among ethnic minority populations. He argued further that there is in adequate evidence to show that empirically supported therapies (EST) are effective with ethnic minorities, suggesting that ethical guidelines for psychotherapies should be modified to become culturally appropriate for ethnic minority people, indicating his acknowledgement of the importance of cultural context in psychotherapy. Although conceptual approaches have identified interdependence, spirituality and discrimination as considerations for culturally sensitive therapy (CST), there is no more empirical support for (CST) than there is for empirically supported therapies (ESTs) with ethnic minority groups.

Hall maintained that there is a chasm between the empirically supported therapies (ESTs) and culturally sensitive therapies (CSTs), and that this is a function of the differences between the methods applied by the two different traditions of researchers.

In my experience as a group analyst and psychotherapist, I feel that what is equally as problematic as the chasm between the two traditions of researchers is the prevalence of uncertainty among ethnic minority social-cultural groups about the forms of psychotherapy that psychologists and psychotherapists speculate as being suitable for ethnic minority populations' needs. This uncertainty is particularly poignant because of the awareness of the ethnic minority groups of the chasms that exist between their own cultures and those of members of other cultural groups who may deign to construct a model or models of psychotherapy for members of other socio-cultural groups.

It has been my personal experience in offering group analytic therapy to people of the Afro-Caribbean and West African ethnic socio-cultural groups that they view with suspicion the efficacy of systems underpinned by the Western model of psychotherapy. For the West Africans it means trusting a system of treatment that is based on the dynamics of the human mind. That is based on the interplay between what is kept in the unconscious mind and what is outside it available to all to understand according to the impulses operating from within them.

Although in the West African perspective it is also a matter of the interplay between the visible and the invisible forces; both the visible and the invisible are externalised. None of the elements is seen in terms of subjectivity; the visible forces are the trees and all the visible creations in the environment and the invisible spirits of the ancestors. With some of the Afro-Caribbean and West African clients, to offer psychotherapy treatment feels like a betrayal of strongly held beliefs, and this includes even the very highly Westernised ones among them. In a recent account of Counselling and Psychotherapy in Nigeria (Bojuwoye and Mogaji, 2013), the authors provide a history of the development of these professions in Nigeria and suggest that:

> Any meaningful future direction in the application of psychological knowledge in Nigeria should, therefore, be towards evolving a hybrid system of practice which incorporates both models (traditional and Western) in mutually beneficial and collaborative partnerships, thus making the advantages of the two systems available for the benefit of the Nigerian people.

I would argue therefore that what is seen as demand for psychotherapy by ethnic minority groups could be based on their curiosity about the model of psychotherapy that is envisaged by psychotherapists and psychologists as efficacious for any ethnic minority group. The non-European ethnic minority societies such our West African societies have their organised and valid knowledge system of healing which is based on sound psychological principles and all our healing systems include some elements of psychotherapy.

Although Chambless and Hollon (1998) said that culturally sensitive theoretical models of psychotherapy have been developed for multiple ethnic minority groups, it is not stated how it was realised that these groups declared a need for this system of treatment or on which criteria their developments were based. I consider this to be an important factor in thinking not only about psychotherapy models but also in considering the credentials of any one constructing a model of psychotherapy who is not an autochthon of the society for which the group therapy model is being developed. This is, I would argue, because only the members of their societies are likely to know enough of the social heritages which form part of their very existence as a people. They know the values behind the norms by which they live and on which their social security is founded and on which their identity as a people is founded.

All West African and others throughout the African continent have their own traditional systems of treating illnesses based on those social-cultural belief systems governing their philosophy of the causalities and treatments of the different illnesses (Moodley et al).

Hence I would argue that there is ambivalence among West African and perhaps also some European ethnic minorities about the efficacy of models of psychotherapy designed for them by anyone who is an alien to their social culture. The proponents of the importance of socio-cultural factors in understanding social illnesses, their cause and cure, emphasise this point.

Experience of the effectiveness of psychotherapy for non-European ethnic minority groups, including West Africans in the UK, suggests that this is an issue in which people's social morality and belief systems play the most important part. In other words, which particular model of psychotherapy is perceived as satisfying the need of a particular social-cultural group? Or what are the socio-cultural circumstances of the person or persons for whom a model of psychotherapy is intended? What type of psychotherapy should be applied to which social-cultural group of people and who is best placed to determine such a model? What language of psychotherapy is spoken to an ethnic social-cultural group?

I would argue strongly that these questions are pertinent because psychotherapy is concerned with issues of conformity with socio-cultural norms including the language, verbal or other forms as in case of the arts psychotherapies which use different forms of art and drama as means of communications. Verbal languages are essential since ultimately even what is acted out has to be made intelligible in the form of language as people's normal means of communications. That is why in my view the value of psychotherapy to any recipients both in terms of the individual within his/her social-cultural ethnic group, and in terms of any social-cultural ethnic group as a whole, depends on the social-cultural contexts. Languages as medium for communication are culturally bound.

So how do we determine whether psychotherapy is indicated, for whom it is needed, and therefore which is the suitable model to employ? The answers, if properly given should address the individual or individuals' social factors. That is those factors which identify him/her as belonging to a particular social-cultural group and governed by specific norms of behaviour and ethical standards.

I will now discuss in more detail the views of the proponents of socio-cultural factors as the pivot on which problems that require treatments with psychotherapy revolve.

Peter Sedgewick (1982) wrote that R.D. Laing said that all the modern revisionists of the psychiatric enterprise – the anti-psychiatrists – take as their starting point a socially deterministic orientation on the nature of mental illness.

In associating social problems that are treated with psychotherapy with the ideological discussions of the anti-psychiatrists, it is in the sense that what are labelled as mental illnesses by the anti-psychiatrists come under the category of illnesses that are distinguishable from those afflicting the human physical biology. By mental illnesses I refer to those social problems that affect emotions, feelings and behaviour patterns. The categorisation of this group of social problems became increasingly a subject of radical groups who questioned the integrity of psychiatric diagnostic techniques arguing that their diagnosing might just be a matter of labelling people that they experienced as awkward individuals. This group cited the practice in the Soviet Union where it was alleged that 'awkward' people were sometimes labelled as mentally ill because their behaviour was considered to be anti-social. They argued that faulty family relationships could be dealt with by labelling the family scapegoat, as it were, as mentally ill. Peter Sedgwick cited further Ronald Leifer, who although paying due credit to the social grounding of medicine as a profession, still insisted that in physical diagnosis and treatment, the term 'disease' refers to phenomena that are unregulated by social custom, morality and law. However, psychiatric concepts of disease refer on the contrary to behaviour, which is subject to the regulation of custom, morality and law. Leifer (1969) wrote that psychoanalysts in various parts of the northern hemisphere, such as North America, are guided in their practices by a metaphorically illustrated map of the mind. It is therefore not surprising that it became necessary to redefine mental illness to reflect what they felt was its correct context in people's social culture in terms of what it is understood to be, its incidence and its management processes.

All this shows the magnitude of the task of determining what is a suitable model of psychotherapy for any social-cultural group given that those social problems which indicate psychotherapy treatments fall into the area of treatments that consider as paramount social norms, social conformity and deviancy, all of which are concerned with cultural identity and cultural peculiarities. Causal factors can only come from the individual's social-cultural network that labels him or her as being ill; the character of the illness or social problem is usually seen as equivalent to anomic cultural behaviour or deviancy. S.H. Foulkes (1964) delineated certain social abnormalities that indicate psychotherapy as treatment option, namely character disturbances, social and relationship difficulties, lack of success in life, different types of inhibitions, neurosis, anxiety states, phobias, psychosomatic disorders.

Thomas Scheff (1966) formulated a set of propositions which he believed made up basic assumptions for a social system model of mental disorder. That is they form the basis for categorising or diagnosing complaints which fall under the category of problems that are not of the nature of physical illnesses. In other words, social problems such as those whose solutions can be found through psychotherapy.

Scheff delineated three conditions which he considered crucial for a sociological theory of mental disorder, namely:

i   The conditions in a culture under which diverse kinds of deviance become stable and uniform.
ii The extent to which in different phases of careers of mental illness the symptoms are the result of conforming behaviour.
iii The possibility that there is a general set of contingencies which lead to the definition of deviant behaviour as a manifestation of mental illness.

The significance of Scheff's three points is that they show clearly that a theory of mental illness is a theory about conditions in people's culture; that in different phases of careers of mental illness the symptoms are the results of deviating from social norms.

Another significance of Scheff's parameters for a sociological theory of mental illness lies in the general ethos of the anti-psychiatry movement of which Scheff himself was an active member and which included Thomas Szasz and Michel Foucault and which was spear headed by R.D. Laing. They emphasised the importance of social context in the labelling of mental illness explored the issues of public provision in the care of the mentally ill.

Taking into account the above arguments, I will now look at the West Africans' belief system, the basis for our philosophy for causality of illnesses and their healing, hence the basis for constructing the appropriate theory that is sensitive to our social culture.

Practitioners in Europe and England all have their own modern maps, each of which emphasises the approach that is adopted by the different psychoanalytic schools of thought. As the analysis of the processes and philosophy of healing of illnesses among West African people would show, our traditional orientation is guided by the type of the map of the mind which is comparable to that which Malcolm Pines (1989) described as being the works of philosophers, dramatists, poets, visionaries and men of religious faiths. That is why in our psychotherapy practice, our healers make use of their knowledge of the physical and the metaphysical elements of our environments. The sensual and therefore empirical, combines with the mythological and the metaphysical elements of our social environments in formulating our treatment approach.

The traditional aboriginal African healers' methods of diagnosing illnesses are based on some culturally meaningful theories about illness. This approach is replicated in other parts of the continent of Africa. For example, as Leslie Swartz (1998) argued, the Zulu tribes of Southern Africa have two ways of categorising all illnesses. One group of illnesses covers those categorised as illnesses which 'just happen' – the *Umkhuhlane*. This category includes such complaints as small pox and influenza as examples. They understand such illnesses as being universal in the sense that they can occur in any society and are amenable to treatment with herbs and barks. In the Zulu tradition, such illnesses do not require any ritual incantations and invocations and displays.

In contrast are disorders understood as diseases of the African people and explained as diseases which occur as a consequence of African cultural traditions, hence they are described as *Ukufa kwa Bantu* and they attract the most attention of the South African traditional healers. This distinction seems to me as that between physical illnesses and emotional illnesses. In other words distinctions between illnesses of the *soma* (body) and illnesses of the *psyche* (mind) which Scheff set out as his three conditions for a theory of mental illness. This suggests that to the Zulu healers of Southern Africa, in the illnesses of the *Umkhuhlane* category, the somatic belong entirely to the realm of the sensory and the visible. The fact that they do not command as much attention of the Zulu healers as do the social problems of the *Ukufa kwa Bantu* category, the physical body, suggest that they hold no mystery for the Zulu traditional healers. I would argue therefore that they are strictly social problems arising from beliefs, ethics of conduct, behaviours and social order of the Zulu culture and as such they are functions of deviation from or non-conformity with the social norms.

However all things considered, it is difficult to have any form of traditional West African healing process that does not include some aspects of psychotherapy.

In my view this is so mainly because the traditional worldview of any West African society is a combination of the physical world available to the senses with the unseen world of the spirits. Therefore the social or group mind perception of reality transcends the individual's sensory level of perception.

Belief in supernatural causality underpins the concept of illnesses and the curative or healing processes. One aspect of the West African cultural tradition – religion – is and has always been the basis for explanation of West African epistemology. Of course things have moved on very much since the Greek philosopher Thale said that all life originated from water and all life returned to water, because he observed in Egypt that crops began to grow as soon as the floods of the Nile receded from the land area in the Nile Delta and because he also noticed that frogs and worms appeared wherever it had just been raining.

But in spite of advances in our knowledge of our social environments and culture, there is still evidence of continuing recourse to mythology in varying degrees in various societies of the world. This fact is exemplified by our characteristic orientations to illnesses and their healing by our West African traditional healers as I have described here.

In other words the socio-cultural context of West African people determines our orientation to illnesses and their healing and also our system for maintaining good health even when we are abroad as here in the United Kingdom and in other predominantly Western cultural societies. I base this argument on the premise that effective psychotherapy is one that is culturally appropriate for those to whom it is applied.

The West Africans' social-cultural attitudes to illness

Attitudes of our psychiatric ill patients reflect our belief and knowledge about our world environment and therefore our beliefs in the causal factors of illnesses. They are entrenched and accepted even in today's world of post-colonialism and its legacy. We therefore feel unsafe with a philosophy of healing with which we are not familiar. Our way of diagnosing illnesses is quite different as is our choice of the appropriate healer who would normally be chosen from among the healers of our tradition. West Africans still reserve their right to choose between our traditional healing methods and the Western world's methods. This is most particularly so in cases of non-physical complaints.

Lambo and Leighton(1963) reported that Africans are ambivalent about European methods of medical treatment and may consult a native practitioner while under treatment in a modern Western method in hospital. Asuni (1973) following a study of the Yoruba people concluded that they under-utilised modern psychiatric facilities. Following his investigation of the Igbos in Eastern Nigeria, Amatu (1973) indicated that emotionally disturbed individuals rarely went to a psychiatrist but instead read pamphlets or popular magazines about the human mind and 'how to solve personal problems'.

This at least is a reflection of the attitudes of the literate Igbos who can read, since only the literate would be able to read the pamphlets. The non-literate members of our societies show attitudes of even more distant associations with the European traditional systems and philosophy for the care and maintenance of the health of people with psychiatric problems.

I can recall personal experiences of these attitudes at the Aro psychiatric hospital when it was necessary to engage the cooperation of the paramount rulers of the compounds from which the patients came to persuade psychiatric patients to accept the prescribed medications. In the first place they attended the hospital with reluctance and the reasons for this attitude were and are obvious.

To start with the Aro village community hospital was the first psychiatric hospital built in Nigeria to treat indigenous patients with what were then the most modern Western psychiatric treatments such as various forms of psychotropic drugs, sedatives, and tranquilisers. In addition to these, electro-convulsive therapy and insulin therapy were among the treatment armamentarium used in the hospital at the time. Many of these treatments were as new to these hospital patients as they were to those in some similar hospitals in the Western world where the treatments were manufactured. Imagine therefore how strange they were to the patients to whom even the idea of such industry was extremely remote. Even most of the staff who were being introduced to these methods of treatments found them strange and unfamiliar and even unheard of in some cases.

Also the milieu in which these treatments were administered was unusual and strange. The administration of treatments was alien to the majority of people involved including the staff who as aboriginals were more familiar with methods of healing and an environment that conformed with traditional beliefs about illnesses and their healing. The hospital and its treatment methods gave the first insight into the wide differences between our orientation to illness as natives of this West African society both from the point of view of learning about these new medicines and participating in administering them as treatments. The opportunity of this experience also gave us brief insight into other worlds and the opportunity to test our willingness to allow these other approaches into our experiences, the patients and the staff as well.

My own experiences can also be categorised into two related aspects. One of these relates to my experiences arising from and connected with my training to become a psychotherapist and is a result of the differences in the social cultures of my country of birth and those in my adopted country, the United Kingdom of Great Britain. The second aspect, however, relates to issues concerning my relationships with my kinsfolk in my country of birth as illustrated in Vignette 7.1 'Reflections on the impact of my training on kin relationships and country allegiance'.

Vignette 7.1 Reflections on the impact of my training on kin relationships and country allegiance

The issues concerning my relationships with my kinsfolk in my country of birth arise from the special method of training to qualify as a psychotherapist as well as from the clinical application of the psychotherapeutic technique in the healing processes.

To begin with, I share the view of those who say that psychotherapy as a treatment option tends to be requested by a certain social class group, the middle-class group of people in the society. This factor is quite apart from the consideration of whether such people in this social group's complaints indicates or does not indicate application of psychotherapy as a treatment option.

My experience during my time of working at the Aro psychiatry hospital in Nigeria as a psychotherapist confirmed to me the notion that people of certain social-cultural groups are less likely to ask for psychotherapy as a treatment option. Added to that factor, my Western approach to treatment by psychotherapy naturally had an obvious cultural bias that militated against the cultural concept of curative factors of my society of birth.

It was my experience that it was necessary and important to keep verbal communications strictly within context. Failure to observe this had the potential leading to the collapse of interactions. That is, the patient may hold back from exploring the issues relating to his/her problems. There were times that I had groups of medical students who were seconded to be exposed to the concepts of psychotherapy practice. With their background in psychology, it was easier to discuss principles of psychotherapy.

However, those of them that were contemplating including psychotherapy practice in their treatment armamentarium brought up the question of the language of the terminologies used in psychotherapy as an issue. This was because the terminologies such as the 'ego', 'self', 'projection', 'denial', 'Oedipal complex' are terms which give the therapist the sense of the working of the mind. However, they are not appropriate as terms for eliciting or interpreting the state of the unconscious. I would argue that this is the case in respect of psychotherapy treatment of people of Western culture as well as those of non-Western culture such as the multi tribal people of the country of Nigeria. My group consisted largely of people who, although they were literate, were however, people of various tribal cultures. They consisted mostly of cultures that spoke and heard different and various tribal cultural languages. Each of these varieties of languages and dialects was different from the Western language used in the training and practising in the Western model of psychotherapy in which I was trained. I am quite aware that even in the clinical practice of psychotherapy of the Western model, the usual practice is to avoid eliciting unconscious thoughts and feelings using such terminologies as 'defence' 'projecting' or 'denying' and so on. The patient may not connect these expressions with or relate them to the corresponding feeling or experiences from which the therapist made the interpretation. In such case there is the risk of the patient becoming confused and even disillusioned.

Most of the issues that I have had with my kinsfolk regarding my training and practising as a psychotherapist had emanated from the differences in the methods of my training and clinical application of theory. Following my understanding of the system of training and practice of psychotherapy according to the traditional system of my society of birth and those of the United Kingdom where I was trained, I locate and identify these in the philosophy of illness causalities and their treatments. My saving grace in this situation however, lies in my habit of regular visits to my homeland of my birth, to keep abreast of events and maintain my acquaintance with people and social activities. When I visit, I am privileged to hear and see how people's daily lives are affected by continuing changes in the world, economic hardships in the developing worlds, hostilities of one religious sect against the other. People of my older age generation ask if I saw their sons where I live. Such inquiries immediately betray the obvious the fact that those who ask such questions do not know enough about world geography. However, more important, is that such question are intended to establish a closer relationship with me; trying to reach me where I am; bridge that gulf between us. I believe thereby that my kinsfolk welcome my visits because of the inherent mutual benefits that we all share from our meetings. I believe also that the camaraderie, spirit of comradeship and friendship which we share during our meetings are evidence of the common bond between us.

That makes it all the more puzzling to my kinsfolk that I continue to abandon them, and spend such long times away in the United Kingdom of Great Britain especially since my retirement. They would remind me of my obvious social standing and position in our society, both within my immediate UmuOla clan and within my esoteric social group of affiliation as well as within our wider social group as the people of the Abiriba Igbo nation.

I cannot pretend that I am immune to these queries from my kinsfolk about my characteristics. At the very least, I do re-assess my decisions in the light of my commitments, my health, my welfare and those of my immediate family and my extended family. I would then consider the merits and demerits of the way that I have chosen to live my life and weigh that against my spirit of patriotism. Another factor which I am obliged to take into consideration is that by choosing to reside in the United Kingdom, I am obliged to delegate some of my social and civic duties to other people in my extended family. It is a privilege and a right of every individual to bear at least some of the social and civic responsibilities of maintaining the society, however onerous that might be.

On balance, I believe that my choice of living in the United Kingdom gives me a wider scope of achieving a balanced lifestyle and wider scope of being of service to myself, my family and my society. I have not fallen behind on any of my personal, social or civic responsibilities. Therefore, I believe that I am as patriotic as I can be. Even given that patriotism is said to be a virtue, it is not the only virtue I would say.

As I stated earlier, healing processes in African societies accord with our cultural beliefs about illnesses which are lacking in the Europeans' healing philosophy and systems of application.

Following his survey of the Igbos of Ihiala, Mbaezue (1975) concluded that the majority of people believed that mental illness was caused by juju, witchcraft or afflictions at a distance by magical means.

Lambo and Leighton (1963) cited an investigation of Nigerian students who suffered mental breakdown while they were studying in Britain, which found that traditional beliefs about the causes of mental illness were not confined to the uneducated people of our societies, but were also widespread among westernised and professional Africans. Evidently, there is an overwhelming reliance on traditional treatment methods because of the nature of the belief in the cause and therefore the cure for illnesses both physical and mental.

Another aspect of our cultural attitudes to mental illness is that all illnesses are presented as manifest bodily symptoms even and including psychiatric illnesses. Patients resist attempts at reducing their illnesses to a psychological level of understanding. This is more marked in neurotic illnesses than in psychosis.

However, according to Lambo and Leighton (1963), a larger proportion of patients in the early stages of psychotic illnesses, up to 95%, put much emphasis on bodily complaints. In many cases especially of neurosis, the symptoms are entirely somatic, consequently rendering the diagnosis of the underlying illness and implementation of treatment problematic. This research may have contributed to widely held views that depressive illness was rare among sub-Sahara Africans. The continuation of these attitudes to illness is confirmed by Oyewole (2013) in Punch Online. Oyewole advocates for a greater understanding of psychotherapy in Nigeria but acknowledges the difficulties:

> This model may not fit appropriately into our situation as it may be difficult to get an African on a couch for the purpose of enabling him or her to freely associate as common practice in the Freudian model of psychoanalytic practice. Our concept of causation of mental illness as often supernatural is usually shrouded in secrecy and expected to be unravelled through divination, irrespective of level of education. Nigerians open up more to someone adjudged to possess supernatural powers to solve their problems using symbolism, divination and incantations to appease the gods. This may explain the relative proliferation of Spiritism-based religious movements in Nigeria.

Certain methods and Western approaches to healing psychiatric illnesses are, then, said to be antithetical to members of our societies. This is the finding reached also by some Western and Westernised West African psychiatrists. They argue that the socialisation processes of our citizens predispose us to lack any inclination to engage in elaborate soul-searching and introspection as people of the Western world do. This psychological predisposition is attributed to what they see as our lack of interest in expressing subjective experiences.

Raymond Prince (1961), who was the principal proponent of this view, concluded that we West Africans are detached from such experiences. He argued further that we do not have, as Europeans do, any sense of subjective causality for illness and that West African patients only rarely establish a clear cut causal connection between their symptoms and their emotional life. Causal factors of illness are by and large *projected* to external factors such as witchcraft organised by an enemy in revenge for a past quarrel over land allocation or similar important issues. Or due to the anger of a god because of failure to make appropriate sacrifices to it. Or as a punishment for breaking a taboo.

All these attributed causal reasons for illnesses may sound incredible and unscientific to some with a more scientific, rational outlook to life than us with our beliefs in myths, magic and spirit of the ancestors. However, the rationality of the more scientifically based societies lies on a different plane of reasoning as has been explained earlier. Nevertheless this does not diminish the value of the systems that we employ based on our cultural beliefs.

The role of the relatives of our mentally ill people in their treatments reflecting our cultural attitudes to illness

Relatives play a significant role in the care of their mentally ill kin. Their involvement begins at the point of treatment planning, that is before the involvement of anyone outside the family such as the healers. This shows how the role of the family is valued. Strong bonds and a strong sense of loyalty exist within our West African extended families. They give loyal support to one another in times of need such as for care and support during illness. In view of the social stigma attached to mental illness there is urgency for the restoration and maintenance of emotional stability. The result of a study by R.O. Jegede (1979) of the role of social-cultural factors in the treatment of mental illness in our societies highlights the role of the relatives in times of illness. It shows and reflects the attitudes of our societies when at least 68% of the patients investigated were accompanied to the treatment clinic by their relatives. Over half of the patients were accompanied to the clinic by only one or two relatives. Six patients were accompanied by four relatives and one patient was accompanied by five of his relatives.

Patients quite often had to travel long distances to hospital clinics for treatments involving physical and mental hardship as well as high monetary expenses and causing anxiety for patients who may have felt that they would be at the risk of breaking a taboo through coming into contact with objects that are designated as taboo by the society. Anxiety could arise when the patient was in an unfamiliar environment such as a Western style treatment milieu like the hospital, away from his/her more familiar village environment.

Many patients rely very much on their relatives for support and reassurances before and after such exhausting treatments as electro-convulsive therapy at the Aro psychiatric hospital. As the author noted (Azu-Okeke, 1992), the success of this project was largely due to the important contributions made by the patients' relatives to the structure of the treatment programme. Patients who were discharged but were not yet ready to return to their homes which were far away from the hospital stayed in the village, cared for by their relatives until they were emotionally and physically ready to go home.

Patients who were suffering from puerperal psychosis and other female patients with babies would not have been able to concentrate on their treatment without the supports and cooperation of their relatives. The relatives cared for the children at night in the village while the mothers slept and rested in the care of the hospital staff. The relatives also gave objective reports on the patients when they went back to the hospital after weekend breaks especially following an introduction of new medication or a change of dosage.

There was a suggestion to create a health care service system with special features such as a guaranteed salary scale for low income wage earners who would volunteer to stay with patients who would otherwise not have any one available to care for them because their relatives could not, or those patients who had no relatives to care for them while they were in hospital for treatment.

Such suggestions however ignored completely the damage that these actions if implemented would cause to the kinship and family relationship values of our kind of society. The role of such professional minders would have done more damage to the patients who would be deprived of the special bond that exists among kin in our society than would have benefitted patients. The therapeutic value of such a bond is one of the curative factors that the contributions of the relatives add to the patients' health care programme in our traditional methods. So it was decided to make every effort to have relatives involved with patients' treatments especially in the extended family culture like ours. In some cases even a neighbour can fulfil this important role where a relative is unavailable to fulfil this role for a patients under treatment.

Since all illnesses are believed to have origin in some force outside the individual and out of the control of the individual himself or herself, stigma is accepted as part of the fate that is designed for those on whom it befalls by the forces beyond the individual's. Every member of the society who holds this belief is comforted by this rationalisation and is protected from feeling ashamed by being ill.

This passage reinforces the argument for the importance of taking into account the socio-cultural context of patients in psychotherapy treatments.

Our traditional West African healers' approach to illness: 'heads they win, tails their patients lose'

The healer's repertoire is wide and varied, in view of the following socio-cultural factors:

- Our belief system that governs our philosophy for the causality of illness
- Our traditional methods of healing our sick

- The roles of relatives in the healing processes of our sick, our traditional psychotherapist brings into play all aspects of his experiences when he/she is in the process of healing.

Hence he can exhort his patients into a state of being 'possessed by spirit'.

The patient would then go into a trance and make utterances which are not always intelligible to everybody but to the healer who would interpret the possessed person's utterances into some sense since he himself possesses some extraordinary power which enables him to understand such utterances. At other times the healer himself may be the possessed person and would go into a trance especially as it may happen that at divination the spirits use him as the medium or vehicle for conveying information about the healing procedures. While in trance, he would make utterances of words and may perform various rhythmic dances as part of his repertoire. Hence, possession is a process in which the patient or the healer or an agent of the healer goes into a trance, and is under the control of a force beyond his or her control.

One of the functions of this process is that by attributing the demand that he/she, the possessed individual, makes on his family, for example, to the controlling power of the spirit, the possessed person gains the support of the possessing spirit for the demand. In other words, it would be assumed that it was the spirit that made the demand through the possessed person as its agent. Therefore the demand should be regarded as legitimate and should be taken seriously and should be met. The process therefore was an aid to marginal individuals since it relieves the patient and even the healer of his/her anxiety and tension about the credibility of the demand made by the spirits through the patient or the healer.

Crapanzano (1977) said that possession also has instrumental functions in that it deals with resolution of conflicts. It also has an expressive function of dealing with identity in that a possessed person sometimes assumes a behaviour which although inconsistent with his normal personality and even opposed to, it is nevertheless allowed.

Such privilege, as in psycho-drama therapeutic sessions, allows the individual to express in a socially acceptable symbolic manner, personality traits that would otherwise remain repressed and unexpressed.

The ritual enactments of the myths of healing and the healers are meant to be awe inspiring and impressive, and they certainly do succeed with their aims in that respect.

This marks a typical approach to our traditional healing methods and differentiates it from those that staff and patients of the Western approach at the Aro psychiatric hospital in Nigeria for example, experienced and still experience.

The relatives of the patients are usually convinced and impressed by the traditional healer's activities and his healing methods. All members of the society being also believers in the society's philosophy for illness causality and healing, also believe in the healing processes that stem from that belief system.

I would say that it is legitimate to argue that the relatives may not have a choice about accepting these procedures since they themselves are complicit with the belief system on which the healer and his healing methods are based. So there is a general acceptance of the authenticity of the healers and the healing system by the society as a whole.

The healers' approach to their healing has therapeutic effects of heightening the confidence of the patients and their relatives in the healer and his healing methods.

They are therefore reassured that their chances of recovering from their ailments are promising. The society that labels an individual as having deviated from the norms of that society is also in a position to determine the person's re-entry into and conformity with the social standards of behaviours.

Another function of the traditional healers approach to their healing practises is its didactic value, as the process also provides opportunity for training experiences to apprentice healers.

Tholene Sodi (1998), gave as an example of a process of our traditional healing, a summary of the approaches of the healers to healing, saying that:

> therapy is based on rituals and a group of symbols and beliefs, some of which are general in scope, while others are more specific to a particular society or ethnic group. The rituals may be peripheral, integral, or, universal in the overall therapeutic strategy. In cases of the peripheral ritual, treatment may be preceded by such performances as a ceremonial prayer to the spirit of the ancestors and offerings of libation for example. In other cases ritual is an integral part of the treatment in which case the patient may be asked to perform a ritual ablution in a river for example and perhaps also, at a particular time of the day or of the month.

The traditional healer is usually a charismatic individual, a good and intuitive psychologist, very much in tune with the peculiar stresses of the culture of the society. He is also able to make blind but impressive diagnoses. His techniques include the use of sacred and magical formulae, gestures and paraphernalia which heightens the suggestibility of his patients as well as adding power to his explicit suggestions.

Raymond Prince however argued that these factors occur in the Western world of psychotherapy as well, but in such instances they are usually recognised for what they are and criticised as unscientific and inappropriate. But they are used to the fullest extent in the traditional West African healing practices. Sometimes, the patients tend to be subjected to a continuous barrage of suggestions at all levels from the most intellectual to the most concrete and primitive. Prince argued that this produces in the patient effects similar to that produced in people when a multiple level of bombardment is employed in advertisement of commercial goods.

The healer would deliberately heighten his patients' anxiety when he feels that it is necessary to do so. For example, if he feels a challenge from his patients to his/her authority over a particular issue, or if he senses a general pattern of challenge to his authority developing in the group. This is because, it is in his interest to maintain an overall air of authority and omnipotence. His social position in his society is among the hierarchy of the elite. It is part of our system of traditional beliefs that people who know the herbs that heal tend also to know the ones that do not. In other words, they also know those that are poisonous. Some such people are believed to be capable of misusing their knowledge there by abusing their positions of trust by doing malevolent deeds. The society would, by withdrawing its trust in such people, and by so doing isolating them from in the community. They are then usually avoided and contacts with them are made by only few people and with great caution.

The belief in the existence of people such as these balances the equation of the good and the bad elements of our West African societies. It explains some of the characteristic approaches of our healers for example when they test their readiness to embark on their healing professions on completion of their apprenticeship period.

Popular methods of treating mental illness

There are at least three most popular methods of treating mental illness among our citizens. In the Southern territories, native practitioners who specialise in the treatment of emotionally disturbed people, inherit their authority for healing as passed down to them by a parent or an uncle. They would then go through a prescribed period of apprenticeship as do all those who are designated as healers. They are obliged to follow a set of principles that overlie actions that they take to intervene in in their healing of illnesses.

In the Northern territories, where the populace consists largely of Moslem religious, inhabitants, mentally ill people are treated by Mallams who are also spiritual teachers and leaders. Their treatment methods include prayers for the relief of the affliction to their patients, amulets with prayers written into them and talisman to wear around the neck, arm or waist especially in the cases of women.

In addition to these two traditional methods of healing, the modern but foreign Western psychiatric methods of healing introduced by Western colonialists are available.

The colonialists calculated that as more people of our societies were being educated, there would be increased demand for Western-type of psychiatric treatments and psychiatric hospitals as a result of increased strain on the existing facilities. Indeed there are many more such hospitals now throughout the country, including the old asylums which have been up graded to provide modern type psychiatric treatment facilities. But there is no clear evidence that demands for psychiatric health care of the Western-type has justified the increase in the provisions of psychiatric hospital facilities for our people. There is also a question of the type of treatment that is preferred by our native psychiatric patients themselves, a factor which goes back to our beliefs about illnesses and their treatments.

As far back as 1972, Torrey warned about the danger of what he called psychiatric imperialism or the assumption that the Western psychiatric techniques are superior to traditional West African techniques of healing. Or even that the Western technique is suitable for our native psychiatric patients.

The Western trained psychiatrists with their set of naturalist beliefs about the cause of illnesses may encounter difficulty or even conflict with our people who have traditional ideas that illnesses are brought by supernatural forces and evil spirits, and that malevolent and evil doers can inflict illness unto a victim.

Conflict between the doctor (or psychotherapist) and his patient arising from ignorance of cultural issues involved can be both on the level of diagnosing as well as on the treating of the patient. Also for a situation between the therapist and his patient, the problem will be even more serious since such cultural factors can be at the root of the patient's psychopathology. The therapist's assessment of his patient's need cannot be adequately made if he lacks the means of understanding what could be the fundamental cause of the patients' problems.

It is interesting to compare the process of the group and the role of the group therapist within a traditional model of psychotherapy with that of the Western therapist.

During the early life of an analytic group, it endeavours to deal with its primitive anxieties by projecting its super ego into the conductor. The conductor of the group normally allows this at this stage in the life of the group as part of the strategy for containing the primitive anxiety. But he works towards the time in the group when the group would modify its super ego components and leadership then becomes ego based rather than super ego based. That means that neither the patients nor the group conductor claims a position of higher authority in the group. In contrast with the role of the Western-type group leader, the traditional group therapist maintains and keeps control of the leadership of the group always projecting himself as the authority figure who is to be obeyed. He never allows himself to be seen in the position other than that of someone who is always right.

He uses direct commands at every stage when he and his patients are together during the administration of medicine, healing rituals, divination sessions, sacrifice procedures and discharge ceremonies. However he gives the patient a continuous assurance that the treatment will make him/her well.

Suppression elements are prominently employed. For example, the healer shouts commands such as 'Stop behaving like a mad man'; 'Don't listen to those voices'; 'Be a man'; and such statements.

Simile, illustrative story, singing, use of sacramental elements such as rituals, magical gestures, and objects that are deemed to represent in the spirit world what is taking place in the material world, are all means employed by the healers to get the patients to endure the barrages and retain attention despite the repetitions of commands.

The belief that the spirits have the same properties and needs as human beings do and can be recompensed and mollified, make sacrifice a very important aspect of the traditional West African psychotherapy practice. As may be designated by divination, sacrifice is set out for the unseen forces of the spirit world of the ancestors, spirits of the forests, spirits of thunder and other spiritual forces of the cosmos. They are expected to accept living or material items such as cockerels, hens, goats, tortoises, eggs, kola nuts, offered as sacramental elements in spirit sense. Each of these elements represents a particular aspect of humanity and all the material elements of human environment. They are used as means of placating and appeasing the spirits. With prayers, singing and dancing, patients experience a reduction in the level of their anxiety.

According to Raymond Prince this is due to the socialisation processes of the West Africans which predisposes them to lacking any inclination to engage in the kind of elaborate soul-searching and introspection as people of the Western world. He attributed this psychological predisposition to the West Africans' lack of interest in expressing our subjective experiences. He assesses us as being detached from such experiences and as having no sense of emotional causality for illness. Prince argued further that as patients we only rarely establish a clear cut causal connection between our symptoms and our emotional life. Causal factors of illness are by and large projected to external agents such as witches, sorcerers and evil spirits.

These Western and westernised psychiatrists conclude that as a consequence the West African psychiatric patient is passive in his relationship with his/her healer as they consider manipulation of the environment. Following divination a patient may be instructed to change his abode or occupation because evil spirits inhabit it and his spirit is restless because he is not living in conformity with his 'heavenly contact'.

Membership of cult groups has some ego-strengthening quality. The operation of cult groups has some elements of abreaction and is also supportive. The patient becomes a member of a new circle of friends who are bound together by the initiation into a common group. They are bound together by joint possession of esoteric lore and secret objects which they feel sets them apart from other people in the society. The sense of being apart from others in the society, and being watched by one's double, ancestors and one's *CHI-neke-(CHI the creator)* strengthens the ego of the cult members.

Prince (1961), however, is of the opinion that increasing the patient's inner strength, like a transference cure, lasts only as long as the association with the cult lasts.

That notwithstanding, while it lasts the patient enjoys the benefit of belonging to a group in a society in which one's social existence is meaningful only within the context of the values of his social groups of affiliations. Furthermore, I disagree with what I see as Prince's misinterpretations as a result of ethnocentric bias. The dynamic factor here in my view is the culture of the projection of one's super ego onto the idealised external force visible or invisible.

Some Western and westernised West African psychiatrists have felt that certain aspects of the psychological profile of West Africans make non-directive and free association forms of psychotherapy all untenable approaches to practice with people of West African cultures.

Prince attributes this to what he called the intense oral orientation of West Africans which according to him is the consequence of a prolonged period of 'intra-uterine' existence by being carried on the mother's back for a long time during the period of the child's infancy.

This is a practice not typical of European nursing mothers' techniques but which is a very popular and common practice among nursing mothers of our western society. As a matter of fact, however, this it is not a prevalent cultural practice in all of our societies. It is a predominant practice among the Yoruba women in the South West region of our societies where Raymond Prince worked and studied the prevalent traditional culture. This predisposes the child to dependency on a relationship with his/her supernatural such as the culture of *projection* of his super ego to the supernatural agents such as the spirit of his ancestors. Or the forces within an anima alienates him/her from subjective attachment to the cause or causes of his illness.

The taboo of discussing family matters with non-kin precludes free association and non-directive group analytic psychotherapy. Traditionally, psychiatric illnesses carry a label of social stigma. Families with a mentally ill member would not allow him to join a group of strangers who would get to know about this family tragedy. Acceptance of the factor of stigma attached to mental illness may be possible under the aegis of our cultural beliefs about illness causalities and treatments, but treating our citizens who are suffering from social problems of mental illness through alien Western methods is what we consider as stigmatising. Usually families keep their mentally ill members in the privacy of their home and seek the service of traditional healers who are usually preferred to Western scientific psychiatrists.

The Western model approach to psychotherapy

The approach of group analytic therapy in the Western tradition to emotional problems begins with the assessment of the needs of the group as a whole in terms of the issues which have caused the members to congregate in the group seeking for something. This may be found to relate to experiences originating from misconceptions and misunderstandings of their experiences of their world in the earlier part of their life with such important people in their lives as their parents. We may then form an alliance with the group, taking the view that these misconceptions and misunderstandings are not unreasonable experiences. If, however, we follow the more traditional theory of personality development and psychopathology we might see this situation differently – as the irrational offspring of autonomous and unconscious fantasies.

The former assessment obliges the therapist to create an atmosphere in which his patients can explore their representational models of themselves and their attachment figures with a view to reappraising and restructuring them in the light of the new understanding that they might have acquired and the new experiences that they have in the therapeutic relationship. To put this in the group analytic context, the group analytic therapist encourages the group member to consider how the current perceptions and expectations, the feelings and actions to which they give rise may be the product either of the events and situations that they encountered during their childhood and adolescence, especially those with their parents. Or else may be the products of what they may have been repeatedly told by their parents.

Foulkes (1964), as I have referred to in other contexts in this work, takes the position that the essence of the individual is social and he develops only in a social context; the individual is only a nodal point in the social network. His view is that the therapist should approach the group in a way which enables the members to recognise that their image or model of themselves and others derives either from past painful experiences or from misleading messages emanating from their parents.

In the West African traditional society, the individual identifies with his social group in an undifferentiated way. He does not matter as much as his group. Foulkes' view of the nature of the human psychology is very much a mirror image of the nature of the traditional West African people. This is so perhaps because the most basic society is that which retains its natural structure and is yet able to advance with time at its own pace. As the Nigerian historian Ajayi (1999) warned us, it is important that no amount of changes to our traditional order as legacies of colonialism should be allowed to alter the widespread concepts that legitimacy to govern is to be based solely on conformity with our traditional customs. This frame of reference should throw light onto the approach and attitudes adopted towards illnesses and healing by our traditional healers.

Our indigenous traditional healers

Foulkes' view is that the therapist should approach the group in a way which enables the members to recognise that their image or model of themselves and others derives either from past painful experiences or from misleading messages emanating from their parents. The circumstances of our traditional social culture means that the misleading message will emanate from our groups of affiliation. The healing process takes into consideration the theoretical position that neurosis and psychological disturbances in general have their origin in disturbed social relationships.

Foulkes' view that the society as a whole rather than the individuals who live in it matter more is in accord with our traditional West African cultural view. However the methods adopted to help people whose social behaviours have deviated from the acceptable norms, in the different societies, vary. Whereas the western psychiatric patient acknowledges that his problem is a result of psychic conflict, the traditional West African can only accept somatic presentation of illnesses as a result of machinations of some malevolent external agent.

This nevertheless does not exclude the element of conflict as the central issue in the consideration of the appropriate treatment process. This remains the prominent issue, between the individual or group and the higher world order of his society. I have argued that it is indeed because of the conflict between his *individual self* and his *group self* that the individual patient or group is placed into dissonance with the society and the label of deviancy attached to the person or to the group as the case may be.

It is the state of conflict between the individual and his/her 'Chi' which takes him/her to the oracle. The difference lies in the nature of the conflict or how it is understood or misunderstood and consequently how it is approached in different societies. In most parts of the Western world of group analysis the conflict is located within the patient himself in his relationship with the world outside in which he lives. To resolve it, the group analyst approaches his patients with the aim of helping them to identify and understand what is happening in their inner world regarding their background, upbringing and development and in relation to their present social network.

If the same patient presents to the West African traditional healer, the healer will approach the conflict from the perspective of events of his environment outside of himself in his endeavour to help the patient to realise how he has incurred the wrath of a force outside himself. In other words he will apply a culturally meaningful diagnostic system and then proceed to treat the condition. The external force is revered and regarded as infallible and the therapist by virtue of his position is never regarded as being fallible either. The relative positions of the two, the patients and the therapists, remain the same throughout the relationship between the group leader and his patients. As I have stated earlier in this chapter, there would never be a stage at which the group members are helped or encouraged to replace the leader's authority with theirs. Nor would the group leaders ever entertain the view that the group knows and should say what should happen in the process of the treatment except to agree with him and accept his assessment of the patient's situation and condition.

This is because of the belief that the cause of the illness is supernatural, spiritual or magical and as such that it is only the group leader/healer that is equipped with divine power to know the right state of affairs and consequently the right course of actions in the processes of healing. The therapist – healer – derives his skill and authority for healing directly from the divine and higher order of forces. He is therefore never deemed to be wrong in matters of the mind/body. His diagnosis is given to him during divination and he, as the agent of the spirit world, relays what he is told by the spirits to the patients and their relatives.

If, however, something goes wrong with the patients'/group's treatments, this would never in any way be attributed to the healer neither as a matter due to his/her inefficiency nor would the healer himself admit to lack of experience. He/she is never fallible or culpable. He/she would never openly admit to that about any aspect of his healing practices. His patients are unlikely to declare any doubt that they might have about the healer's efficiency since that would be construed as questioning the integrity of the higher power. This collusive relationship effectively substantiates the cultural belief of the society and creates an all-win situation for the healer; *head he wins and tail his patients lose.*

Yet our society believes in, trusts and accepts this unique relationship with our healers because it represents an important link in the chain of the social order of acting according to our socio-cultural beliefs.

The indigenous healer fulfils two essential functions as integral parts of his healing processes: He identifies the particular experience presented by his patient and diagnoses it. He relates the patient's experience to some meaningful cultural theory which enables him to reintegrate the patient into the fold of his community. This after all is the purpose of psychotherapy. The patient's complaints may appear and sound vague to untrained ears. However, by narrowing down the cluster of symptoms and complaints through certain assessment devices such, Divination, Reading of cowry beads, Guided finger prints on sands, Bones and Dreams interpretations, the healer will analyse and identify his/her patient's problems. He will then be in a position to give a culturally compatible diagnosis of the problem.

Tholene Sodi (1998) points to five psychological principles that underlie this health care system:

1. The indigenous healing system is a process of many steps which begin even before a healer is consulted. The patient's family will first arrive at a 'primary consensus' on the hypothetical meaning of the illness and hence the choice of the healer appropriate to deal with it. The relatives' decision to consult the indigenous healer is in one sense like seeking a secondary consensus from the wider community. This on its own merit reassures the patient and his family that the patient's illness is of concern to others too. When the patient's family are involved in this way the healing process can no longer be a matter between the patient and healer only. It would involve also the patient's relatives, the spiritual powers, and other community members.

2. Suggestion is another psychological principle which is applied because (a) the indigenous healer's power is believed to be rooted in his link with the spirit world; (b) the use of secret formulae when treatment is given; (c) the healer may aim at strengthening the ego of his patient by telling him/her the story of his past successes in dealing with similar cases as that of his patient; (d) transferring of illness and evils to objects according to

their evaluated worth in relation to what they represent in terms of ills and any manner of affliction. This technique is based in the belief that there is a force that would enable the healer to pass the affliction within the ill person to some object such as a lizard, toad or another lower creature which would then be the afflicted victim while the human patient, it is believed is then relieved of his afflictions.

3   According to Turner (1973), the symbolism of rituals provides a representation of the dominant social and moral order as well as appeal to the senses. The symbolic aspect of healing rituals allows the patients to locate their illness and its cause within their cultural framework, symbols being related to such fundamental issues like birth and death which operate at unconscious level.

4   Possession, which I have discussed above, is the fourth psychological principle of healing which Tholene mentioned.

5   The fifth psychological principle of healing is the characteristic nature of the African community itself. Tholene highlights this as being like as a therapeutic milieu in which 'the equilibrium of the traditional life pattern is as yet relatively undisturbed'. Its four basic elements, namely rehabilitation, permissiveness, democratisation and communalism, remain as natural parts of the community network awaiting a systemic re-channelling towards therapeutic ends.

It is interesting that Yalom (1970) includes these four in his inventory of the therapeutic curative factors which are inherent in therapeutic community hospitals for people with non-medical social problem.

Yet there are people who actually take a severe and negative view of the contributions of the traditional West African healers to psychological medicine. For example, Dr. Motlana Sodi in his submission to the Gauteng legislature in 1998 calls attention to the fact that there were still many people complaining that they were expected to continue to believe in mumbo jumbo while the West had moved into CAT scans and advanced sonar for diagnoses. They complained they were asked to believe that dried up bones of monkey's ankle can provide diagnosis.

Indigenous healing nevertheless has its own adherents who refuse to allow it to be ridiculed as mumbo jumbo. Tholene Sodi is one of those who value indigenous healing as an organised and valid knowledge system based on sound psychological principles.

The West African traditional healers' orientations of causality of all illnesses includes elements of mysticism, and unseen forces. In that way the somatic is not separated from the psyche in the diagnosing of illnesses. Healers therefore look for factors in the ill person's psycho-social environment which may have contributed to his illness.

Sodi argued that the indigenous healing system is a comprehensive method of healing in that it treats the body, the social and also certain psychic states such as guilt and anxiety. It needs to be elevated to a true status that is at least comparable to that of Western psychological medicine in its own right.

This West African system of belief in healing has implications for the social individual. The fact that an individual entertains fear of sorcery or witchcraft can only be a matter of course. Such fear is within all members of our society as one of the mysterious experiences of our lives. As a result of being conscious of this we employ every means available to us, to defend ourselves against any threats of evil and or sorcery that we fear may be militating against our welfare. This includes being suspicious about a form of treatment which we feel is contrary to our beliefs about the treatment of the particular kind of illness or social problems.

The issue of psychotherapy practice as I have discussed it here, presenting both the West Africans' and the Western world's such as Britain and the North Americans' perspectives, gives rise to other important issues that command attention especially if we are to address adequately the question of its application for ethnic minorities such as ourselves in West Africa. This is particularly so if we are to address the specific cases of those societies within 'Nigeria'. At the start of this chapter I stated that there is increasing feeling among psychologists and psychotherapists that demand for psychotherapy among ethnic minority populations is increasing. At the same time and from the perspective of a group analyst and psychotherapist, I feel that what is more prevalent among the ethnic minority populations is uncertainty about the efficacy of this form of treatment for them. They are more curious about what it is about especially against the background of the differences in the conceptions of illnesses, the governing beliefs about illnesses and their treatment methods in different cultures.

Hall (2001) mentioned three issues that arise in the consideration of psychotherapy for ethnic minorities. One of these is the issue of *empirically* supported psychotherapy; that is therapy treatment whose efficacy can be empirically verified but which is not available to ethnic minority groups. Hall suggests following his psychotherapy research with ethnic minorities that there was not adequate evidence that empirically supported therapies (ESTs) are effective with ethnic minorities.

This situation raises the second issue which is how ethical or not it is to provide non-empirically supported therapies for ethnic minority groups.

The third issue which arises in considering psychotherapy for ethnic minority populations is that of the concepts on which culturally sensitive therapies could be determined. This raises a different issue of how to make psychotherapy efficacious for ethnic minority groups thus raising the question of whether there is a need for a generalised psychotherapy approach that would accommodate all who need psychotherapy including the ethnic minority groups.

According to Nagayama Hall, conceptual approaches identified three factors to be considered for culturally sensitive therapy, namely interdependence, spirituality and discrimination. However, one of the suggestions also made was to include ethnic minority groups with the empirically supported therapy groups in a scientific investigation of the efficacy of psychotherapy. This, it is argued, would also help to determine whether psychotherapy approaches could be generalised.

In continuance for the search for an appropriate psychotherapy for ethnic minority groups another impetus for psychotherapy research was suggested with a consideration of economics. It was estimated that the ratio of the African Americans in the United States was increasing and would within fifty years rise from 30% to 50%. It was expected that many ethnic minority persons would want psychotherapy services that are culturally sensitive.

If however, culturally sensitive therapies are not developed, many ethnic minorities may not seek psychotherapy, it was argued. Consequently psychotherapy services would elude a growing market for it. In other words the reason why psychotherapy should be provided to the African Americans ethnic minority group is so that the providers of psychotherapy could take advantage of the financial benefits expected to accrue from the practice. To emphasise a point that I have already made in this chapter, psychotherapy needs to be culturally sensitive in order to take into consideration the important factor of the social context of the problem for which psychotherapy is sought for as the solution. Considering the idea of providing psychotherapy treatment for the principal reason of not losing out on the financial rewards that such activity is calculated to potentially promise would, I would argue, be regarded as unethical and immoral in our West African societies.

There are other voices that echo the same concern about what is the appropriate therapy for ethnic minority groups. This has led to the development of different models of culturally sensitive therapies since persons from one cultural group may require a form that differs from psychotherapy for another cultural group. Furthermore, there may be cultural variations among persons within a cultural group which would necessitate additional modification of the type of psychotherapy interventions needed.

This emphasis on the relevance of cultural contexts in the tailoring of psychotherapy to specific groups, that is creating culturally sensitive psychotherapies, is not intended to suggest that context is irrelevant in empirically supported therapies.

There are also ethnic minority groups among Europeans as there are among non-Europeans, yet this is not clarified in making the claim. Even within the different psychotherapy practitioners, there are different groups such as the Humanistic psychotherapists who would legitimately claim that the basis for their practice of psychotherapy take into account context and spirituality.

However, socio-cultural contexts are as yet to be adequately investigated in research into empirically supported therapies and I question how such investigation would be conducted and what would be the criteria by which the efficacy of each culture's model would be authenticated.

As Sodi has stated earlier our system is a tested model of psychotherapy, a comprehensive method of healing that treats the body the social and also certain psychic states such as guilt and anxiety.

The suggestion made by S. Sue et al. (1991) that the ratio of ethnic minority groups in America seeking psychotherapy was increasing omitted to mention how this group indicated their need for psychotherapy or their reason for their need, nor was there any indication of how *any* particular ethnic minority group had indicated a need for psychotherapy.

Nevertheless, there are in each group's planning for suitable psychotherapy models for its people, considerations for those socio-cultural factors which are at the root of problems that require psychotherapy for solution.

Even given the common factor between culturally sensitive psychotherapies and empirically supported psychotherapies the two approaches nevertheless are based on different orientations to illness and their treatments. The empirically supported therapies would be those which are practised following the guidance of the metaphorically illustrated map of the mind that indicates the areas and boundaries of the mind and with areas illustrating the *id, ego* and the *super ego* and emphasising the origins and depths of their strata. This is a logical supposition since as Malcolm Pines wrote, twentieth century psychologists were employed to draw such maps to guide psychoanalysts and psychotherapists in their more modern maps.

The cultural context of this approach makes it more appropriate for an empirically supported psychotherapy suitable for people of European and North American cultures. Approaches to psychotherapy for West African ethnic minority groups, however, are informed by the orientations of men and women of religious faiths, philosophers, poets, visionary men and women and dramatists of their societies. Similarly psychotherapy for different ethnic groups should also be appropriately culturally sensitive. I therefore share the view advanced by Barlow (1996) and Beutler (1998) that from an ethical perspective it is important to appreciate and recognise diverse cultural groups and acquire the ability to work effectively with them.

Some argue that culturally sensitive psychotherapies need to be empirically supported if they are to survive under the scrutiny of managed care. This is to suggest that culturally sensitive therapies have to become empirically supported therapies. I would argue that that suggestion needs to clarify what in reality it means for a therapy to be empirically supported, since empirically supported therapies are culturally sensitive therapies for the particular ethnic minority group to which it is applied.

The criteria for the test for empiricism are those socio-cultural norms of the society by which boundaries between order and disorder are determined for the society. The criteria include also the system of beliefs which demarcate between the accepted socio-cultural norms by which our orientations for the causes and healing of illnesses are formed. These therefore form the basis for testing the efficacy of our systems of healing.

Chambless and Hollon (1998) argued that among the European Americans, empirically supported therapies are treatments that had been demonstrated to be superior in efficacy to a placebo or another treatment.

I therefore share the view with those who argue that from the ethical perspective, it is important to appreciate and recognise diverse cultural groups and the ability to work effectively with them.

C.C. Hall (1997) had argued that whenever there had been inability to work effectively with diverse cultural groups, it had been characterised as cultural malpractice.

It is emphasised, according to APA Office of Ethnic Minority Affairs, that ethically it is a mandatory requirement and in the USA it is also part of accreditation requirements for training programmes to provide psychological services that are responsive to the needs of individuals of diverse backgrounds.

These service guidelines are applicable to psychotherapy research. The interests in the provision of guidelines for the providers of psychological services to ethnic, linguistic and culturally diverse population were intended to present general principles which were aspiring in nature and designed to provide suggestions to psychologists in working with ethnic, linguistic and culturally diverse populations.

The guidelines by the American Psychological Association (APA) (1990) recommended that psychologists should recognise ethnicity and culture as parameters in understanding psychological processes and that cultural differences regarding language, family, community, religion, spiritual and sociopolitical issues be understood and respected.

All these various efforts from the various researchers including the American Psychological Association Office of Ethnic Minority Affairs to find suitable approaches to the provision of appropriate psychotherapies for ethnic minority groups emphasise the awareness of the necessity to take into account the prevalent social-cultural factors of each particular ethnic minority group.

Secondly, the degree of eagerness to make culturally sensitive therapies empirically supported therapies, that is therapies that are scientifically testable for their efficacy, seems to imply that only therapies which are scientifically testable can be considered as suitable forms or efficacious forms even for ethnic minority people.

It would mean that the criterion of cultural belief which mitigates cases that would otherwise be regarded as inefficacious would no longer serve that purpose. For example such criterion as our belief that the native psychotherapist is never wrong because the efficacy of his therapeutic practices comes to him/her through the powers of the spirits. In other words the cultural factor which is the nucleus of a people's identity is disregarded as irrelevant in the formulation of a culturally sensitive therapy approach, sacrificed at the altar of scientifically verifiable efficacy.

Yet I would argue that there is no universally verifiable efficaciousness of psychotherapy as there is no provable uniform method of application of psychotherapy techniques. I would argue further that the effectiveness of psychotherapy is not statistically measurable.

This sets up a contradiction which can be resolved in one of two ways. One of these is to discount the value of an important aspect of our cultural beliefs in the formulation of an appropriate therapy model, but this is a sacrifice that West Africans would feel too culturally expensive to make. What would be fairer is for colonialists to recognise the damage that they have perpetrated through their cultural imperialism and the colonisation of our West Africans psyche. We could then freely enjoy the benefits of our heritage unfettered by the parameters of the alien colonial values.

There is however an eagerness to embark on more research programmes to explore methods of achieving competences in multicultural counselling and already this had been adopted by the American Psychological Association Division 17 (Counselling) and the Association of Multicultural Counselling and Development.

D. W. Sue et al. (1996) argued that the multicultural counselling competency that is most directly relevant to psychotherapy research involves developing appropriate intervention strategies and techniques.

S. Sue (1998) suggested that what he called dynamic sizing, which refers to skills in knowing when to generalise across cultures and when to individualise, is an important component of cultural competence. This is not to be seen as stereotyping; it is simply that knowledge of a culture is an asset that provides us with a context in which to understand our clients. That in turn would enable us to determine the differences in individuals of the same culture within a group.

Sharing an experience between a therapist and his clients may help the therapist to empathise with his clients but he would however need the expertise of a culturally competent therapist to realise the limitations of his experiences. For example, although the therapist and his clients may have shared a common social experience such as racial discrimination, the therapist would be less likely to experience his/her racial discrimination in a similarly intense degree as his client, especially if the client is a member of an ethnic minority group and the therapist is a member of the majority group. In West African psychotherapeutic models the relationship between the therapist and his clients is always kept on an unequal basis by both parties, the healer-leader, and the patients-the-lead.

The issue of psychotherapy for ethnic minority groups needs to be put into correct perspective. It is in my view, and in agreement with Thomas Scheff, an issue, unlike in physical health matters, about conditions in people's culture that show that in different phases of careers of social problems the symptoms are results of deviating from social norms. Thus, psychotherapy for ethnic minority populations needs to be both empirically supported and culturally sensitive (Hohmann and Parron, 1996). Sue et al. (1999) however, did not indicate the basis for that need other than to say that culturally sensitive therapy models were to be developed so that psychotherapy would reach the growing market for it due to the need for it by the African American ethnic cultural groups. I would suggest that there is an economic reason for encouraging the development of some psychotherapy models that are considered to be suitable for ethnic minority groups. There are no clearly identified categories of psychopathological evidences among the ethnic minority groups that indicate the need for any model of the psychotherapies for them.

I do agree however that where psychotherapy is indicated for any group, it should be a culturally sensitive model. That is the model that reflects the culture of the person or persons deemed to 'need' psychotherapy. Consequently, if there is to be advance in research in the field of psychotherapy with ethnic minority groups all should contribute their knowledge: to suggest that societies like ours should abandon their model of psychotherapy practice would, I argue, be another example of cultural imperialism that subjugates our traditions and which amounts to departing from our customary traditional ways of healing.

Yet there is optimism among researchers that despite the important differences between the Europeans' models of psychotherapy some of which are empirically supported, and culturally sensitive models such as those of West African societies, there could be a comprehensive method of healing that treats the body and the social. It may be that time will come when our cultural beliefs will change to scientific empiricism then we as a people would no longer be affected by the destructive consequences of colonialism which sought to change the way that we treat our patients who need psychotherapy. The author has experienced the two models of psychotherapy although not because of actual need for psychotherapy treatment but only as incidence of fortuitous occurrence that is training.

When considering the implications of the colonial relationship with our societies to our utilisation of psychotherapy services as ethnic minority groups within the wider world communities, I suggest they are influenced by the concept of globalisation of colonialism which has become the focus of international relationships between the Third world military and economic powers and the First world military and economic powers so called.

Globalisation of colonialism has moved the focus of the explanation for colonialism from such clichés as the White man's burden of having to go to civilise the savage Africans. As Subhabrata Bobby Banerjee and Stephen Linstead (2001) argued, what is now given by the First world powers and economies as explanations for the new global colonialism is that we are in the era of an emergence of a global culture of universalised economy in which all societies including the third world share equally the world resources. That is what the colonialists want us to believe. However, Banerjee and Linstead see the so-called global colonialism as simply a process that marks the transformation to a culture of consumption. In fact a culture of consumption so serious that it is dealt with by attacking countries which have the required resource under any pretence to exploit them of the commodity at any cost. I mentioned earlier in this chapter that the length of time of exposure to colonial rule varies and with that variation is the intensity of dehumanising and degrading treatment of the colonised people to preserve their presumed air of superiority over the colonised. When they leave, they leave behind the legacy of uncritical acceptance of their culture, the consequence being that the victims of colonialism begin to put into practice during their self-rule some of the inherited colonial characteristics such as overthrowing a government by coup d'état under some pretence or the other. Clearly however the true reason is usually serving self-interest in the same way as the colonialists. The irony is that when this happens the colonialist will describe such action as the barbaric action of uncivilised people.

I feel that it is necessary to point out that I am aware that the process of writing this book has aroused more emotions of discontent with the processes of the colonisation of our West African societies and I believe that I have made this fact clear throughout.

However I fear that there is danger of my over-reacting and giving the impression that everything about our lives under colonialism spelt gloom and doom and that all was lost. In spite of my reactions reflecting the feelings aroused by colonialism and taking into consideration the totality of my experiences of the colonial regime, I have some positive feelings arising from aspects of the colonialists' ruling activities that I would consider and accept as positive in that they made positive contributions to our well-being.

The difficulty and hesitation in acknowledging the positive contributions as readily as I have pointed out the negative aspects of the colonial regime stem from the fact that the positive legacies are fewer and they were not bequests made purposely to benefit us. Any benefits that arose for us as a result of such actions were incidental and not a result of the colonialists' altruistic intensions toward us. For example, and as Emmanuel Obiechina (1975) pointed out, the provision of British education was motivated by utilitarianism. It was because the spread of the Christian religion, the introduction of modern institutions and the running of modern government required a cadre of literate men and women. Education was therefore geared towards producing clerks, teachers, evangelists and artisans who represented personnel for the lower rank of the civil service and commercial enterprises, teaching and missionary work.

It is ironic that it was because we were given English literal education that I am able now to question the many anomalies and injustices that were done to us by colonialism. It was this opportunity that we were granted by the same colonial regime that made it possible for our political activists, especially those who brought their expertise from the American liberal educational academies, to challenge the British colonialists at their own games proving that even the British colonialists' capitalism contains the elements for its own destruction.

However in relation to the specific issue of psychotherapy for an ethnic minority social-cultural group like our West African societies, for example, two specific issues should exercise the mind. The first concerns the type of the relationships that our societies experienced under colonialism. That must have direct bearing on our trust or lack of it in the capacity of the British colonialists to construct a suitable model of psychotherapy for our type of society.

The second issue concerns the nature of our social, political, economic institutions and our belief system particularly about illnesses and their cure. We need to consider the impact of our cultural traditions on our psychic formations;

how the different cultures of our different societies influence our intra psychic formations. We need to consider the part that they play in shaping our thoughts about ourselves and our environments.

Believing as I do that our cultures influence our psychic formations then cultural analysis should be a prominent feature of group analytic training if therapists are to be properly equipped for treating people of ethnic cultures like ours. In the present days' clinical settings of increasingly diverse cultural contexts, the necessity to address such issues becomes even more urgent. In thinking about specific impacts of colonialism on our intra psychic formation, the question arises of what such impact might be in the circumstances of being ruled by a foreign power, such as the British colonialists and of suffering subjugation of one's own traditional culture by the colonialists and imposition of their alien ones on us.

The impact of experiences of colonialism can and does vary with the length of time that a people undergo the experiences. Following such episodes of colonialism, what might then be the impact on intra psychic formation of the experience of being nominally ruled by one's own people but only within the parameters set by a foreign power, and in many cases ruled not by the government chosen by the people of one's own country but by a government that is acceptable to the foreign power? Of course that condition is not usually openly stated in that tone but is made clear that unless that was the case, certain unfavourable consequences would result. The world was never told that Iraq would be invaded because the world's most militarily powerful country wanted to take control of its petroleum mineral. The world was told that the existing regime was evil and had amassed weapons of mass destruction and therefore was a danger to the world. Since securing the control of the country's petroleum resources, and installing the government of their choice there have been no more mention of weapons of mass destruction. Nor has there been any mention of the cost of such act of colonial oppression and barbarism either in terms of the loss of human life which remains ongoing, or in terms of the social unrest within the country and the thousands of displaced people both within the country as well as the thousands of Iraqi people living in foreign countries in misery as refugees.

Indeed how would such a situation augur with C.C.I. Hall's suggestion made earlier here that whenever there has been inability to work effectively with diverse cultural groups, it had been characterised as cultural malpractice. In what context then can we place the impact of our experience of colonialism on our intra psychic formation which creates a situation in which even when we are ostensibly ruling ourselves, we do so only within the parameters set by the foreign colonial powers of the British?

When they colonised and ruled us directly we suffered subjugation of our traditional cultures. What can we imagine would be the impact on the intra psychic formation of the people of Iraq be after such experience of colonialism? Can they be expected to trust people who had no regard for their social culture and traditions to understand enough to be sensitive to their cultural context? I would argue that they cannot trust such important aspects of their lives to the care of such people whose sole interest was exploitation of their natural resources. It is then not surprising that there should be difficulties over such sensitive issues as cultural traditions, which mark the identity of people, between us, the Iraqis and any other society that has had the misfortune of being colonised.

For more than half a century, people like myself lived under the control of such government and suffered from most of the adversities that I have discussed in this chapter and indeed in some of the other chapters. One of the consequences of such political setting can highlight how problematic it can be to contemplate applying the Western model of psychoanalytic treatment to our West African citizens given the ideological differences between them concerning the issue of illnesses. I would argue that for me the route of the Western (British) model of Group analytic psychotherapy or the route of my traditional group therapy model which relies on the dynamics of the forces of the unseen spirits of the ancestors rather than on the dynamics of the equally invisible forces of the mind, is an issue of understanding the therapeutic merits and demerits of each model and therefore determining how far and in which direction to go at any one time under given circumstances.

The distinction between the two experiences however is that the training in the Western model of group analytic psychotherapy introduced the realm of the dynamics of the invisible human mind or the awareness of the dynamics of the psyche to me and to it. This was a novel experience for me given that there is no and never has been a concept of the 'mind' which is accepted as potentially capable of manifesting the forces of consciousness, semi-consciousness, sub-consciousness and unconsciousness in my West African cultural experience as in the Western context of the mind. All functions attributed in Western culture to the forces of the mind, are in my West African culture attributed to the human anatomical organ, the heart – 'Obu' or 'Obi'. The mind is an invisible phenomenon whereas the heart is a palpable and visible biological organ as is universally known. Events are understood to occur as a result of the interplay between such visible matter as the heart and the invisible or metaphysical objects such as the spirits of the ancestors.

Nagayama Hall optimistically argued that despite the differences between empirically supported therapies and culturally sensitive therapy researches, the approaches need one another for the field of psychotherapy research with ethnic minorities to advance.

Empirically supported therapies approach without a cultural context is not likely to be relevant to culturally sensitive therapy researchers and ethnic minority clients. Nor is culturally sensitive therapy likely to become part of mainstream psychological science without an empirical basis. I would argue therefore that given the vicissitudes of our life during and following colonial rule over us, it is difficult to envisage in the near future, factors in the lifestyles of West Africans which will provide a suitable socio-cultural environment that would enable provision of both empirically supported and culturally sensitive therapy models which can serve the therapeutic needs of all ethnic minority groups as well as all other groups that require psychotherapy.

It is important that some formula is not adapted for any particular group of people purely in order to benefit from the economic opportunity of benefitting from the presumed market for psychotherapy for African American ethnic minority group.

These are the issues that have been brought into the forefront of my thoughts following the outcome of my research relating to the specific issue of the place of psychotherapy and group analysis for people of our West African social culture, like the author.

Reference list

Ajayi, J.F.A. and Falola, T., ed. (1999) *Tradition and Change in Africa: The Essays of J.F. Ade Ajayi*. New Jersey: Africa World Press.

Amatu, H.I. (1973) 'Problems of clinical practice in Nigeria', Paper presented at first African Regional Conference of the International Association for Cross Cultural Psychology, Ibadan, Nigeria, April 2–6.

American Psychological Association (APA). (1990) *Guidelines for Providers of Psychological Services to Ethnic, Linguistic, and Culturally Diverse Populations*. Available at http://www.apa.org/pi/oema/resources/policy/provider-guidelines.aspx.

Asuni, T. (1973) 'Social, cultural and environmental determinants of psychiatric services in Western Nigeria', Paper presented at the Annual Convention of the American Psychiatric Association, Hawaii, May 1973.

Azu-Okeke, O. (1992) 'Experiments with Nigerian village communities in the dual roles of western psychiatric treatment centres and homes for indigenous Nigerian inhabitants', *Therapeutic Communities*, 13(4), pp. 221–228.

Banerjee, S.B. and Linstead, S. (2001) 'Globalization, multiculturalism and other fictions: Colonialism for the new millennium?', *Organization*, 8(4), pp. 683–722.

Barlow, D.H. (1996) 'Health care policy, psychotherapy research and future of psychotherapy, American Psychologists', *Annual Review of Psychology*, 51(10), pp. 1050–1058.

Beutler, L.E. (1998) 'Identifying empirically supported treatments: What if we didn't?', *Journal of Consulting and Clinical Psychology*, 66, pp. 113–120.

Bojuwoye, O. and Mogaji, A. (2013) 'Counselling and psychotherapy in Nigeria: Horizons for the future', in R. Moodley, U. Gielen and R. Wu eds., *Handbook of Counselling and Psychotherapy in an International Context*. New York: Routledge, p. 48.

Chambless, D.L. and Hollon, S.D. (1998) 'Defining empirically supported therapies', *Journal of Consulting and Clinical Psychology*, 66, pp. 7–18.

Crapanzano, V. (1977) 'Introduction', in V. Crapanzano and V. Garrison eds., *Case Studies in Spirit Possessions*. New York: John Wiley and Sons.

Foulkes, S.H. (1964) *Therapeutic Group Analysis*. London: George Allen & Unwin Ltd.

Hall, C.C. (1997) 'Cultural malpractice: The growing obsolescence of psychology with the changing U.S. population', *American Psychologist*, 52, pp. 642–651.

Hall, G.C.N. (2001) *Multicultural Psychology*. New Jersey: Prentice Hall.

Hohmann, A.A. and Parron, D.L. (1996) 'How the new NIH guidelines on inclusion of women and minority apply: Efficacy trials, effectiveness trials, and validity', *Journal of Consulting and Clinical Psychology*, 64, pp. 851–855.

Jegede, R.O. (1979) *Aro Village System of Community Psychiatry in Perspective*. Unpublished Paper.
Krause, I. (1998) *Therapy Across Culture*. Thousand Oaks, CA: Sage Publications Ltd.
Krause, I. (2014) 'The complexity of cultural competence', in F. Lowe ed., *Thinking Space: Promoting Thinking About Race, Culture and Diversity in Psychotherapy and Beyond*. London: Karnac, pp. 109–126.
Lambo, T.A. and Leighton, A.H. (1963) *Psychiatric Disorders Among Yoruba: A Report From the Cornell-Aro Mental Health Research Project in the Western Region, Nigeria*. New York: Cornell University Press.
Leifer, R. (1969) *In the Name of Mental Health: The Social Functions of Psychiatry*. New York: Science House.
Mbaezue, M.J. (1975) *The Search for Sanity in Igbo Land: A Survey of Traditional Methodology in the Treatment of Mental Illness in Ihiala Division and Its Environs*. Unpublished Honours thesis. University of Lagos, June.
Obiechina, E. (1975) *Culture, Tradition and Society in the West African Novel*. African Studies Series 14. Cambridge: Cambridge University Press.
Osuji, O. (2006) 'The purpose of psychotherapy, secular and spiritual', March 8 in Nigeria Village Square Series 32. Available at http://www.nigeriavillagesquare.com/index.php?option=com_content&view=article&id=2575&catid=583&Itemid=233&allposts=1.
Oyewole, A. (2013) 'Psychotherapy, culture and mental health', *Punch Online*, November 28.
Pines, M. (1989) 'Group analysis and healing', *Group Analysis*, 22(4).
Prince, R.H. (1961) 'The Yoruba image of the witch', *Journal of Mental Science*, 107, pp. 795–805.
Scheff, T. (1966) *Being Mentally Ill: A Sociological Theory*. Chicago: Aldine.
Sedgewick, P. (1982) *Psycho Politics*. London: Pluto Press.
Sodi, T. (1998) 'Indigenous healing not "mumbo jumbo" valid knowledge system', *Children First*, June–July.
Sue, D.W., Bingham, R.P., Porche-Burke, L. and Vasquez, M. (1999) 'The diversification of psychology: A multicultural revolution', *American Psychologist*, 54, pp. 1061–1069.
Sue, D.W., Ivey, A.E. and Pederson, P.B. (1996) *A Theory of Multicultural Counselling and Therapy*. Pacific Grove: Brooks/Cole.
Sue, S. (1998) 'In search of cultural competence in psychotherapy and counseling', *American Psychologist*, 53(4), 440–448.
Sue, S., Fujino, D., Hu, L., Takeuchi, D. and Zane, N. (1991) 'Community mental health services for ethnic minority groups: A test of the cultural responsiveness hypothesis', *Journal of Consulting and Clinical Psychology*, 59, pp. 533–540.
Swartz, L. (1998) *Culture and Mental Health: A South African View*. Cape Town: Oxford University Press.
Torrey, E.P. (1972) *The Mind Game: Witch Doctors and Psychiatrists*. New York: Emerson Hall Publishers, Inc.
Turner, V.W. (1973) 'Symbols in African rituals', *Science*, 179, pp. 1100–1108.
Yalom, I.D. (1970) *The Theory and Practice of Group Psychotherapy*. New York: Basic Books.

Chapter 8

Bringing it all together
Looking back, moving forward

In this chapter I will discuss and reflect on my research, taking the opportunity to share with readers how the various parts link together. As a practising group analytic psychotherapist, I used my analytic training and work with patients in a variety of settings to reflect throughout on how my explorations into my life in different cultural settings have impacted on my identity.

When I began preparing for the book, I had a hypothesis, based on my own experiences and those of my fellow Igbos. I intended to explore this and possibly to prove my point. As time went on, I became less interested in trying to prove my hypothesis and more committed to understanding how I, as an Igbo man, and many of my fellow Igbos, had been affected by British colonialism – and particularly the impact that colonialism has had on our identities. However, I kept in my mind the original hypothesis, which was as follows:

> the British colonial ruling policies on the group of West African societies and states that they named as the country of 'Nigeria' had the effects of rupturing and dislocating the cultural institutions and cultural traditions of the societies with detrimental consequences.

Accordingly, I began with an introductory chapter that gave an account of the issues that I intended to explore including reflecting on my own perspective. That is, my personal experiences of living under the colonialists' regime, including a particularly very sensitive and conflict-arousing experience that caused me severe anxieties and identity confusion during my formative years, namely the shooting of a bird.

In this chapter I argue that the experience of colonialism had such a great impact on my life that it became imperative for me to embark on a journey of exploration to discover my root as it were, to find my authentic origin and a social network within which I can be identified as a human being that must belong – because it is only within the context of my social network that I can be identified as a human being.

Hence, although I started the book with my own stories, I deemed it essential that many other relevant people, that is, those who are also part of my social network, should give their own stories too so that the book can present a balanced and objective panoramic view of my life in the context of my cultural origin. I considered this relevant because I am who I am by virtue of my cultural origin and the way that life has impinged on me, and I have acted as a human being.

There were times when I was confused about who I was, and what my life was about in my Abiriba Igbo society, proud of its cultural traditions. These were issues that threatened my identity as a member of the society and made me to feel alienated from my social-cultural groups. I argued that this situation arose because of the presence of the British colonialists, reflecting their ruling policies for our societies, including coercion of children like myself as well as our parents, as they were made to feel compelled to deviate from our traditional ways of acculturation. The chapter discussed my method of approach to the book and following that, it addressed colonialism, exile, cultural and individual identities.

The chapter acknowledged the importance of contributions of other citizens of our societies, in particular those of the West African novelists. It also introduced the social and political structures of the Igbo societies and people and gave an account of the British education system imposed on us. It introduced the processes that our societies adopted in an effort to cope with the emotional and social traumas that resulted from the social conditions to which we were subjected.

In the second chapter, I elaborated on colonialism in the specific context of our societies and on how that affected our lives. For example, its implications for our cultural identity vis-à-vis the exilic conditions of living to which we were subjected. These explorations involved making enquiries into our social history and politics and our oral traditional culture characterised by a face-to-face system of interactions. I explored the social and political conditions of our societies before the advent of colonisation, during and after, together with an exploration of our identity in the context of our traditional education system, our religious beliefs and our languages. This provided the parameters for assessing and comparing the changes that resulted as a consequence of the type of the ruling policies that the colonialists adopted for us.

In an indirect way, this process revealed the patterns of some colonialists' own cultural traditions, especially in the fields of education and religious beliefs.

Effectively therefore, I could look at the nature of the relationships between the British colonialists and ourselves, including a consideration of the psychosocial aspects of the lives of people of essentially two diverse cultures: ours (the natives) and the British colonialists.

I elected not to continue to be shrouded by the widely maintained illusion that there is a country of Nigeria. Of course nominally there is a region of the world known as Nigeria created courtesy of the British colonialists Amalgamation Act of 1914. I have chosen to resist working under the colonialists' created illusion that there is a place, a land under a particular sovereignty or government inhabited by a certain people or within definite geographical limits. My reason for such rejection is that in the area that was placed under one sovereign rule the several independent countries did not choose to be deprived of their own cultures and traditions, seeing themselves as independent societies within the continent rather than as parts of a geographical entity created for administrative convenience. I regard the circumstances of unilaterally pronouncing so many autonomous and independent states as one united country as making the legitimacy of such arbitrary action a subject for scrutiny. Yet it remains a widely held assumption, albeit predominantly outside its confines than within it, that 'Nigeria' is a united country. My position is central to understanding my account of my personal experiences of the colonial regime in my own Igbo society, such as the conflicts that arose for me, and their consequences for the type of social interactions that I, as well as other youths of the time, had to endure from the colonialists' regime. Principal among these being those that arose for me during my formative years and their implications for my future life aspirations as an Abiriba Igbo youth and the processes of achieving them.

Embodied in the British ruling policies were the types of social relationships that they instigated which changed the whole ethos of our social life. One example was the conflict that arose from my fear that because some of the principles of the Christian religious traditions I had been converted into militated against the cultural traditions in which I was being brought up by my parents, my extended family and our wider society. These conflicting social values had the profound consequence of threatening my freedom to celebrate one of our important traditional cultural rites of passage (see Vignette 1.1).

I therefore perceive colonialism as a political ideology of domination of a people relatively less militarily and economically powerful by another of superior military and economic power. In this particular instance, the British imperialist colonisers.

It is my conclusion that a great urgency developed in our desire to recover our heritage, a very compelling factor that led us to take a risk and adapt to some of those colonialists' cultures that we considered not too militating against our own way of life. That was done as a strategy to recover some of what we were losing through being alienated from our cultural heritage. It was natural, even pragmatic, that we had to adapt in order to survive our exilic social conditions.

Colonialism created conditions that forced us into economic dependency. We were forced into economic production systems that were unrelated to our native economic needs.

Then there was the issue of language. I proposed that language distribution within different racial groups was an important factor to be examined. In an effort to broaden the range of languages, it was considered that the invention of a common Yoruba vernacular through the instigation of the missionaries and based on the dialect of the largest of the tribes (Oyo) would be an added advantage, especially as it had with it the compelling prospect of enabling the Yoruba bible to be printed. In the interest of their own religious missions, the missionaries who formed part of the colonialists' entourage exerted some influence in the societies. For example, the missionaries were concerned with the sizes of the different community groups. They were interested in having one large community group which would have the advantage of providing a large captive audience for conversion into the Christian religious faith. By that process they hoped to hasten conversion more quickly than if the different communities were in smaller groups with their own different dialects.

Similar efforts were made in the Northern Nigerian territory of the Hausas and Fulanis and in the southeastern regions of 'Nigeria' by the Igbo people to repeat this process.

Concerning systems of government, I concluded that the policy of colonialism, which is totally oriented to 'state' type societies, should be seen in the context of our West African societies as an external interest factor that militated against successful and productive engagement with our societies with their characteristic attributes of 'civil' societies. Given these circumstances our civil societies were under-represented in decision making, as the colonialists were concerned only with their own interests. The nature of this inter-relationship has imprints of the different preconceived ideas held by the Western world about Africa, which were testified to by the political theories of Max Weber (1930).

I observed that there was a pattern or correlation between the age generational population and their experiences and impression of colonialism, and as I stated in Chapter Five, there were those who were old enough to experience the effects of British colonialism, that is, the period of their occupation, as well as experience the values of the legacies both material and historical that they left for us. There were also those who because of their age category and social status experienced only the legacies that were bequeathed because they were born when the colonialists had departed. Their experiences of colonialism were limited to the institutions left by the British, such as schools to continue literacy education in the English language, dispensaries, recreational clubs, churches, and even some opportunity for higher education abroad. Those who did not experience what went before, such as the treatment that our traditional rulers had to endure, the humiliation that people who did not behave according to dictates of the colonialists had to endure, could not fully understand why some others did not share the enthusiasm for what they saw as virtuous about colonial legacies. As the younger age generations members of our societies did not have other experiences to compare with our history before, during and after the colonial regime, they could not fully evaluate the effects of colonialism on our societies. Although they may know that in the north 'sabogari' means 'strangers' quarters', they might not understand why and how they were regarded as strangers in the country of their nativity.

This group's experience on the values of colonial legacies were further complicated by the illusion of their high value in material terms. The over-estimated evaluation of our colonial legacies at the expense of our lost heritage culminated in some delusions of grandeur. This group could not do more than empathise with the frustrations of the older age generational categories such as the author who also experienced first-hand the consequences of the colonial policies.

I believe that this was an important factor that had bearings on the responses given by this age generational category of participants in both group discussions and interview responses as shown in Chapters Five and Six.

Yet citizens of the older generations are left to rue the cost to our dignity, our pride and our heritage of these material legacies so highly valued by our younger generational groups. These younger people were oblivious of the culture of discriminations, inequality of distribution of economic resources, coercions and loss of freedom to practice our cultural traditions.

The practice of reserving the best social resources for the benefit of those who occupied privileged positions in the social hierarchy continued after the departure of our colonial rulers and the emergence of our own native rulers. Like the colonialists, our own rulers assumed positions of importance but mostly for their own personal benefit. This meant that like the colonial rulers before them, they encouraged and maintained a social culture of inequalities in which the elite groups ignored the legitimate needs of the poor of the societies while they greedily enjoyed the resources of the land. They reserved the best social resources for themselves while the majority had little or nothing to live on, just like when the colonialists were ruling us. Having themselves been part of the deprived groups in the society during the colonial era, they were tempted to satisfy their own personal interests first and foremost before caring for the interests of the wider societies. This may be interpreted as natural instinct of self-preservation, or as merely emulating their predecessors who kept the best that there was for themselves except that the colonisers looked after their own kind, whereas our native rulers looked after themselves and since we also practice a culture of nepotism, they looked after members of their extended family too.

This attitude raised many questions in the minds of most people in our societies. For example, that if strangers had come to exploit us of our resources, and we were helpless to stop them, we should console ourselves that they are our native rulers who are now exploiting the resources which partly belong to them too. Of course this philosophy was not always satisfactory enough to everyone sufficiently to persuade people to accept the status quo. It was perhaps the strong feelings against this social condition that led to the first of the coups d'état that the societies of 'Nigeria' have suffered. People in groups or as individuals take any opportunity that they feel to be available to them to get to the position that would enable them to exploit the nation's resources for themselves.

There were and there still are areas, especially in the capital cities, where most of the colonialists lived in relative comfort, areas which were and still are designated as government reserved areas (GRA). These are for privileged people, equipped with comfortable facilities, houses and other social amenities in abundance, while the majority of our citizens (some of them in states of abject poverty) fend for themselves as best as they can. They may engage in anti-social behaviours such as participating in corrupt practices, which is endemic and widespread even among the so called elite groups who use their privileged positions to further their own interests.

Those ruling the country were now chosen from among the literate groups drawn from among the graduates of the schools of the British system of education and according to the norms that govern British cultural practices.

Literacy had never been the criteria for ruling in our precolonial societies, nor were our traditional systems of rule based on the acclaimed British democratic principles. Neither could the British system of rule as applied to our societies be said to have been truly democratic even allowing for the fact that at their native homeland there were also some social inequalities.

Documented evidence from my research findings of the lives of the societies and states that came to be grouped together during the colonial era as the country of 'Nigeria' showed (and discussed in Chapter Five) that each one of the states was an independent and autonomous entity. They were not under any centralised government, especially not 'Ndi Igbo', the people of the Igbo nation. Yet the formula for centralised system of governance that was bequeathed to us was recommended to us as the most suitable to govern ourselves.

It is an ethnological fact that we were members of different ethnic and cultural groups within the proximities of certain geographical boundaries in the West African region off the North Atlantic Ocean. The different indigenous societies of the different territories were often as much at war with one another as they were at peace among themselves, but they also had mutual respect for one another's sovereign right to exist independently. However, the British educated members of our societies of all levels often seemed intent on defending their privileged position of being educated. They would argue that those who seemed not to value the type of education that they themselves had received were merely crying sour grapes because they for one reason or the other had not been privileged to receive British education. Hence this aspect of British rule was credited with some merit by some sections of our societies and created some controversies among our people.

The colonial rulers themselves did not really succeed in their time to rule us, they only succeeded in exploiting the country by oppression, coercion and what I would describe as a system of psychic colonisation, which induced 'Couriferism' – the attitude of uncritical acceptance of everything British or European as being better than any of ours. Here again I observed that in my group of participants, there were different perceptions of the effects of the British occupation to our prospects as a people, with variations between the different age generational groups. Hence there were those who idealised the colonialists cultures not only as did the Black Victorians but even the latest generations following the departure of the colonialists. For some of the members of this group, the height of their passion for defending what they saw as the virtues of colonialism was such that they were sometimes hostile to any suggestions that the colonialists ruling policies were in any way detrimental to the interests of any one in any of our societies.

In the same vein some of the recalled memories of some of the interviewees and in group discussions revealed such cynical attitudes as that British education was designed to turn the natives' attentions away from our cultural traditions and values.

An important aspect of my book concerns the connections between people's social-cultural network and their identity, including my own. I have discussed the definitions of culture and identity in the context of their general usages, examining identity formation in the context of our traditional education system, our religious beliefs and our languages as means of acculturation – acquiring our traditional culture as a people in our own right. I discussed how differences in languages can represent differences in cultural traditions and cultural identity; since languages are peculiar to their social-cultural origin. I moved onto the importance of language in psychotherapy and in group analytic culture, for example, where one of the most vital factors that come into the process of the training and clinical practice is language that is used to communicate feelings, especially as psychotherapy and psychoanalysis have their own special languages, which convey special meanings.

I examined the issue of language and multiculturalism in the therapies and discussed how cultures are guided in the forming of words that make up their languages by different factors in their environments, hence different cultures have different names for the same thing. Unfortunately British colonial educational policy treated and held in contempt our native languages and afterwards they were neglected and omitted in the curricular. Consequently we did not receive literacy education in our own languages as the colonialists preferred English and others such as French, German, Latin and Greek rather than any of ours. I referred to Frantz Fanon who had also expressed his view concerning contempt for our native language in his psychoanalytic examination of the relationship between the Black people and the White people where and when the two races are in the presence of each other. He had said that Western bourgeois racial prejudice regarding the Black man and the Arab is a racism of contempt; a racism which minimises what it hates – the black people.

Notwithstanding this, I also acknowledged the efforts of the British colonialists to make it possible for us to become literate even though that was in a language foreign to ours. It has to be said that it is a language that is internationally used and also internally, amongst our different societies and it has had the effect of breaking the psychic insularity that was characteristic of our traditional education. In the process, it substituted a cosmopolitan and mobile psyche according to Emmanuel Obiechina (1975).

I also pointed to another benefit that we derived from literacy in English which is that by learning such a cosmopolitan language as English, more people were provided with a common language to use in our different native groups who all spoke their own languages. Thereby greater physical mobility and broadening of the social as well as psychological outlook was encouraged.

I pointed out the importance of our West African writers who were able to bring back to our consciousness our heritage that we were losing to the colonisers. Ironically we were able to recover our consciousness of the risk of sustaining such loss because of the benefit of literacy in English by those who were privileged to be so literate. They were also able to educate those who could not read for themselves the writings of our culture carrier writers.

Those writers who had the courage to attempt to write for us in some of our native languages were discouraged by being mocked most painfully by their own people as well as our colonisers who encouraged and egged them on. That it was possible for this situation to occur is testimony to the degree of effectiveness of the colonialists' coercions and indoctrination forcing us into the corners that they wanted us to be in our societies.

For writings to be of value as means of disseminating knowledge and information, there have to be people equipped with the ability to read them. In other words there have to be literate people since literacy mediates between the novelist and the reader and makes the rapport possible. The chapter goes on to discuss the context in which different societies of the world construct words that create the formation of their languages. Related to this is a discussion of the exilic social conditions that resulted from the type of the social relationships that emerged as a result of the British colonial ruling policies. I look at the social and political structures of our societies and how these aspects of our social network are involved in the formation and development of our identity and therefore how the dislocating and rupturing effects of the colonial policies came to be to our detriment.

The contributions of the 'Object relations' theorists, including Fairbairn (1952), Guntrip (1969), Winnicott (1965) and Balint (1975), were also pointed out in this chapter as they argued that the primary motivational drive in man is to seek relationship with others.

Considering the importance of religion in our society, the chapter examined the effects of our colonial relationships on our religions, education, and the impact of these effects on our identity as a people. I explored the contribution of the Christian missionaries to the destruction of our traditional religious beliefs and institutions and concluded that it was necessary to adopt a processes of 'mourning' the loss of our traditional social-cultural environments, our heritage, in an effort to cope with the social conditions that were brought about by the colonial policies, especially the exilic social conditions.

Having provided a socio-historical background for my research, I then embarked on what is one of the most important parts of my research for the book: Talking to my Peers – the importance of shared experiences

Since I started to work on my hypothesis, I have had an occasion to share what I aimed to achieve in writing this book with some students studying for the Master's degree in Intercultural Psychotherapy. On introducing my topic one of the students asked me whether there was anything left to be learned about colonialism. I wondered at that point whether the question arose because the student had read everything written about colonialism or whether it arose from the possibility that in fact she knew little about the subject of colonialism. One fact soon became evident however, that all her knowledge about colonialism did not include any personal experience of a colonial regime. I later realised that unlike the author the student was a citizen of one of the so called First World Societies, one of those who colonise other societies of less military and economic power.

I allowed myself to assume that all that she knew about colonialism therefore did not include any personal experience of being colonised. As she belonged to the world of the colonisers, one of the groups of the world societies who whatever else their ethical standing on humanity and human rights, acquisition of capital wealth and expansion of empires attract higher value for them. I of course come from a different background, one in which I could not take my human rights for granted because my society was under the colonial regime which considered individual's right not a right but a privilege to be granted by the grace of the colonising British imperialists.

There were many questions to which I needed answers which I could not expect to come from the very people who had colonised our societies and in the process had created those questions by creating the circumstances of their colonial policies, at least not if I expected to receive unbiased and objective answers to my enquiries. Rather, I felt that a more reliable source of answers would come from those people who shared the same social history such as I did.

That was because, from the beginning of their adventure of colonialism the colonialists were satisfied that the 'end' – the acquisitions of our natural resources and expansion of their empire – by means of exploitations and subjugations of the exploited people, justified the means that they adopted to achieve those ends.

I needed to know whether my own experiences were only an individual's nightmares or in fact experiences of realities that could be supported by other people of our cultures who also shared the history of the colonial times, so they might provide similar experiences as mine. Or provide different experiences of the same social situations that were created by the same interventions of the colonialists in our societies. Or even and perhaps for reasons of differences in individual peculiarities or idiosyncrasies, prove to be different experiences.

I wanted to explore the validity of my original hypothesis, that colonial rule was instrumental in the ruptures and dislocations of our social and cultural institutions, by focusing my attention to this by including both those who were not old enough to have experienced life during the colonial era as well as those who were. In Chapter Five I give an account of the methodology that I adopted and described how I selected participants to respond to the pilot study questionnaires and to take part in interviews and focus groups. The outcome of my exploration was a revelation of wide and varied experiences of life during the colonial era in our country as well as at the time of post-colonialism – so called. I analyse and reflect on these findings, and give some examples of their experience through direct quotes in Chapter Six.

In Chapter Seven I move to exploring the implications of my findings for the future practice of psychotherapy, specifically for the application of a Western model of psychotherapy, or what has been referred to as the empirically supported therapies (ESTs) for non-Western cultures or ethnic minority cultures.

I include West Africans' cultures among the ethnic minority groups since I would argue that those cultural groups which fall outside the mainstream Western European and the North American cultural groups fall under the minority group of users of psychotherapy of the empirically supported models.

Psychotherapy of the Western European and North American models is still predominantly the preserve of the middle classes both in terms of the language used in the application of treatment by this method and in terms of the theoretical orientation which forms the basis for practice. The description ethnic minority as I apply it here is in the sense that in the Western European and North American empirically supported therapy practices would classify people of my West African culture and indeed people from a numbers of other cultures. I base this line of argument on the differences that exist between Western European and North American social cultures and my West African social cultures, and indeed as well as some of the East European and South American social cultures whom I would argue would also fall under the categories of ethnic minority cultural groups.

The Western European and North American models of psychotherapy practice as I discussed in Chapter Seven have been developed from quite different orientations than those which inform West African psychotherapy practitioners. Hence psychotherapy practices which do not predominantly follow Western European and North American cultural orientations fall into the categories of unrecognised models of the minority groups whom, it is assumed, are therefore in need of the correct type which should conform with the requirements of empirically supported types of therapy.

The models of psychotherapy practiced by ethnic minority groups such West Africans are of course based on models of therapy practice which correlate with the system governing our belief in the causes of illnesses and hence the processes of their treatments and healing. I have had the benefit and the pain of being brought up in two very different and often conflicting cultures. This, together with my experiences at the Aro hospital and in my training and practice as a group analytic psychotherapist leads me to the conclusion that all psychotherapy needs to be intercultural psychotherapy which respects and pays close attention to the socio-cultural context of both client and therapist and does not presume superiority of one model over another.

General conclusions

My study has been a journey into the time before, during and after the advent of the colonisation of the West African territories that were collectively named 'Nigeria' by the British colonialists. The history of our societies can be retraced from time long before the British colonialist came to settle and to leave us a legacy of incoherent social institutions. It is generally accepted that humanity originated in Africa some two to three million years ago. The precolonial Africa was a place where different societies existed each reflecting different cultural traditions and systems of government. My study examined the state of the political organisations of our African communities in general, tracing it to two broad categories of the 'state' and the 'stateless' societies and discussed the chances of the formation of 'state' type societies in at least some parts of the continent. In this regard the factor of low population densities and the production of relatively small economic surplus contributed to the hindrance of the formation of state type societies and, as a consequence, most of our African societies were stateless societies at the precolonial times.

As became evident from the findings of the type of relationships that existed between our societies and the colonisers, the Western mentality of societies as essentially of 'state' types was generalised to include such expectations on our societies as well. That not being the case resulted in us being classified by the Westerners as mainly primitive societies with primitive cultures and ideas.

However, in spite of these denigrations, we were a people competently able to develop political systems that were adequate and suitable for our needs. We were also able to develop our own system of law and justice to maintain order and civil liberty according to our needs. Also we were able to develop our own system of representation which made it possible for all citizens to feel included as members of their societies.

Most of our larger stateless societies combined to become even larger ones. My study also considered the essential characteristic features of our societies' social structures such as kinship and lineage systems based on an extended family structure. In the specific case of my Abiriba people of the Igbo lands, I elaborated on the relationship between this kinship system and the characteristic collective responsibility for our social and ego development from the cradle to the grave through the system of the age groups of affiliation. I also explored the implications of this for the Africans' ability to trace their ancestry since ancestor worship is an important traditional cultural practice and is built into the Africans' system of belief including most importantly the structure of the African religion.

West African societies have not deviated from the fundamental principle pattern of our kinship lineage and ancestor worshipping tradition even today. The tradition remains the foundation of such important social institutions as religion, politics and jurisprudence. It is the binding link that holds social and kinship relationships together in our West African societies that make up what was given the name of the country of 'Nigeria'.

As I have consistently shown in the process of exploring the hypothesis, my starting point had been to understand why and how things came to be what they became. That has of course included how I myself came to feel the way that I felt about myself in the society that I was raised and knew as my place of origin and my social network.

I have come to understand that some of the reasons why I had felt like an exile in my own native environment had been because of such colonial legacy as our being *infantilised* as a people through the colonial ruling policies.

Such legacy included also the consequence of what amounted to the colonisation of our psyche, which rendered us to state of self-doubt in ourselves as a people. This effectively meant that the only reality that we came to accept was based on what I had referred to here as 'Couriferism'. That is an uncritical acceptance of all European values as superior to our own native values.

Yet there are people in our societies who see only the good things that White man did for us. The education system that provides us with the means of communicating with the world communities, hospitals which give us alternatives to our native system of healing, different outlook to our life and different sense of values, setting different targets for us to aspire to.

These members of our societies who think in this manner are quite justified because of their experiences of the history of our societies. They grew up to see these things, which to them exemplified nothing other than virtues. This was also against the background of our now dislocated and ruptured cultural traditions by the policies that were applied to our societies by the very powers to whom the credit is attributed for the cherished legacies that they had bequeathed to us. These members of our societies are not aware of the price that our societies had paid for these legacies.

The fact that these bequests, such as British education, medical facilities, recreational clubs and even the prevention and eventual abolition of such inhuman social practices as the killing of foetus that followed the firstborn in instances of multiple births, were seen by the members of the society of different generation such as the author, as coming with heavy price, did not diminish their nominal values.

Such legacies have remained a valuable bequest in to us in their own right. It is especially so to the generations that were oblivious to what had been lost.

I concede that my own colonial legacies have included some virtuous heritage such as my British education and my professional education, both of which have combined to equip me with the ability to explore the source of my demons and so enable me to lay the ghost that had hitherto haunted me. As a psychotherapist, I have been obliged to reflect on my identity, my emotional reactions and where possible to consider the origins of such reactions. As a group psychotherapist my knowledge of how societies are formed and change and how these changes impact on group members has been invaluable in helping me to stand back and to be more aware of the importance of understanding one's socio-cultural history as well as the here-and-now whilst acting as a group facilitator.

It has been from these positions that I have advanced to my present hope of contributing to the recovery of the heritage that we had lost to colonialism. At the same time I would hope that my story and that of my fellow Igbos will contribute to the evolution of a psychotherapy that can truly call itself intercultural.

I am aware that it is important that I retain what I have achieved in spite of the odds against me vis-à-vis: my experiences of the detrimental effects of the rupturing and dislocations our social-cultural institutions and our traditions.

I am aware that my approach to my enquiry betrays some prejudice against colonialism, and therefore I have tended to emphasise the detrimental colonial activities towards us that have indeed blighted our lives as I have written in the chapters here. Sadly colonialism remains, hidden perhaps under the guise of sometimes well-meaning interventions from more powerful countries, sometimes less well-meaning and to do with acquisition of power and of the resources of the colonised.

However on balance I have to say that in my frustration and confusion that arose from the attack that I felt on my integrity from the time of my formative years and which consequently, prompted my embarking on this enquiry, my attitude was primarily to defend against what and where I identified as the source of those frustrations and confusions. These were also what and where I believed to be the source of the degradations, subjugations and abuses of our integrity as a people. It has been with this frame of mind that I had viewed most aspects of our colonial relationships and their consequences in negative light and with much bias. This was often in spite any positive values that they might have had for us and in some cases in denial of the merits that they had.

At the very least I viewed them with suspicion arising from the fact that the whole approach of colonialism and colonial policies were characterised by inhuman approaches towards us, the colonised people, as a whole and to me in my particular circumstances first as a youth and then as a growing teenager. It was an approach that it seemed was to be of necessity ruthlessly exploitative, regardless of the consequences of that to any one, its end justified any means by which it was achieved.

My journey continues with greater clarity of purpose and intention because I know now where I am and consequently I can chose where I am going. I feel that the result of my exploration of my hypothesis has led to my recovery of my own intellectual lethargy and stupor, which had hitherto reversed my priorities of what were more important in my life starting from my life as an Abiriba youth and then as an Abiriba man of the Igbo nation. In reality that meant to fight for the perpetuation of communion with our ancestral spirit by fighting for the freedom and liberation of my African societies from the grips of colonial oppressions and its legacies. This I will do in the firm belief that I with my ancestors – the dead, my living kinsmen and women and even those that are yet to be born will all unite to rebuild our shrines that have been destroyed by the circumstances of the exigencies of the colonialists' ambition. This is possible because I know now where I am and therefore where I am going.

He who does not know where he is cannot know where he is going.

Throughout my years as a psychotherapist working mainly in the 'West', I have become more aware of the existence of the *'unconscious'*; the *'mind'*, a phenomenon that I have said in Chapter One (regarding the importance of language) is not recognised in my traditional social culture in the same sense that it is in the Western culture and in the concept of its meaning. By the discovering of the existence of the phenomenon the *'mind'* and its working mechanisms, I do now understand better the power of my own *'subjective self'*, the existence of which I had denied by projecting it to the powers of the external forces of the spirits of my ancestors and other metaphysical forces all of which form one part in the interplay between the metaphysical and the visible forces that constitute our belief system.

I am aware now that I had projected my subjective power, *'my super ego'*, to the white colonialists as a result of their coercive method of rule.

All of these culminate for me in more awareness of myself and put me more at ease with myself because I now know what forces have played their parts in my life.

These forces are those that have blighted both my traditional West African social culture and traditions and had been at play in moulding my Western British colonial cultural values.

Reference list

Balint, M. (1975) *The Doctor, His Patient and the Illness.* New York: International University Press.
Fairbairn, W.R.D. (1952) *An Object-Relations Theory of the Personality.* London: Tavistock Pubs.
Guntrip, H. (1969) *Schizoid Phenomena: Object-Relations and the Self.* New York: International University Press.
Obiechina, E. (1975) *Culture, Tradition and Society in the West African Novel.* African Studies Series 14. Cambridge: Cambridge University Press.
Weber, M. (1930) 'The protestant ethic and spirit of capitalism', in W.J. Mommsen ed., *Max Weber, German Politics 1918–1920.* Translated by M.S. Steinberg, 1984. Chicago: University of Chicago Press, p. 77.
Winnicott, D.W. (1965) *The Maturational Process and the Facilitating Environment.* New York: International Press.

Index

Abiriba Igbos 12–15, 41, 70, 89, 92, 100, 149; age generational categories 9–12, 15, 79–82, 142–143; naming traditions 70; *see also* methodology
Achebe, C. 8, 42–46, 66
African Traditional Religion (ATR) *see* Christianity
Ajayi, J.F.A. 124
Amatu, H.I. 111
American Psychological Association (APA) 131, 132
Aro psychiatric hospital 1, 111–113, 116–117, 118
Asuni, T. 111
Atkinson, P. *see* Hammersley, M.
autoethnography *see* methodology
Azu-Okeke, O. 62, 116

Balint, M. 22, 70, 146
Bamgbose, A. 68
Banerjee, S.B. 133
Barlow, D.H. 130
Benton, T. 66
Berlin, I. 7
Beutler, L.E. 130
Black Victorians 7, 26, 27, 28, 29, 30, 54, 65, 144
Bojuwoye, O. 18, 106
Brown, D. 22

Campbell, J. *see* Kapur, R.
Casely-Hayford, A. 28
Chambless, D. L. 107, 130
Christianity 2, 9–12, 67, 97, 142; and ATRs 46–55, 98–100
Coleman, J. S. 42
colonialism: and black-skin racism 30, 37–38, 102; and ego identity 8, 27–28, 37, 76, 122, 152; exile within homelands 4, 5–9, 21, 25–29, 35–36; perceived benefits of x–xi, 64, 88–89, 97, 99, 134; psychic colonisation 29, 38, 71, 144, 150; *see also* Achebe, C.; country of 'Nigeria'; Couriferism; education system; healing; Igbos and Igboland; language; psychotherapy; religion
Conklin, H.C. 82
Conton, W. 44
country of 'Nigeria': disunity of 17–18, 29, 78, 86, 96, 102, 140–141; formation of 2–3, 19, 29, 79, 102, 140–141; independence of 18, 68, 97–98, 103; and psychotherapy 105–106, 111–116, 128; *see also* Aro psychiatric hospital; Hausa nation and culture; Igbos and Igboland; Yoruba nation and culture
Couriferism 7, 28–29, 36–39, 144, 150; *see also* Casely-Hayford, A.
Crapanzano, V. 118
Crowder, M. 46

Dalal, F. 2, 4
d'Ardenne, P. 4
Diagne, P. 48

education system: British 16, 29–30, 40, 41–42, 45–46, 63–64, 76, 97, 101, 134; traditional 40–41, 51, 88; *see also* language; religion
Ejiofor, Pita N. O. 16
Ekwensi, C. 42, 45
Elias, N. 22–23
Ellis, E. 4
Erikson, E.H. 35

Fafunwa, A.B. 67
Fairbairn, W.R.D. 22, 70, 146
Fanon, F. xi, 4, 8, 30, 59, 64, 145

Foulkes, S.H. 34–36, 109, 124
Freud, S. 22, 28, 70, 115

Gaarder, J. 34
group analysis 4–5, 34, 59–60, 83, 123–125, 135–137; author's experience of 19, 61–62, 95, 106, 128; *see also* Foulkes, S.H.
Guerrero, G. 25, 28
Guntrip, H. 22, 70, 146

Hair, P.E.H. 67
Hall, C.C. 131
Hall, G.C.N. 105–106, 128, 136
Hammersley, M. 82
Hausa nation and culture 2–3, 142; and language 68
healing 1, 5, 15; and African theories of illness 109–111, 115, 121, 122, 125, 127, 148; psychological principles of 107, 110; traditional healers 117–120, 121–122, 125–128; traditional vs Western methods 111–116, 120–123, 123–128
Hegel, G.W.F. 22
Higgins, R. 75, 82
Hohmann, A. A. 132
Hollon, S.D. 107, 130

Igbos and Igboland: author's identity and experience 9–15, 17, 61–62, 73, 75, 76, 112–114; historical background 2–3; impact of colonialism on 6–9, 17–19, 30–31, 36, 42–46, 70, 73–74, 95–97; and language 59–62, 66–67, 68, 76, 91; peer perspectives 73–74; socio-political structures 23–24, 45; *see also* Abiriba Igbos; healing; methodology
Isichei, E. 16
Isizoh, C.D. 49

Jegede, R.O. 116
Johnston, H. 37, 39

Kant, I. 22, 66
Kapur, R. 4
Kenyatta, J. 16–17
Krause, I. 105

Lambo, T.A. 111, 115
language 57–59, 63–71, 90; English 29–30, 44, 45–46, 59, 64–69, 76, 90; indigenous 29–31, 45, 64–65, 67–69, 99; *see also* psychotherapy

Leff, J. 66
Leifer, R. 108
Leighton, A. H. *see* Lambo, T.A.
Le Roy, J. 35
Levtzion, N. 48
Linstead, S. *see* Banerjee, S.B.
Lipsedge M. *see* Littlewood, R.
Littlewood, R. xi, xii, 2, 62–63
Lowe, F. 4

Mahtani, A. *see* d'Ardenne, P.
Mbaezue, M.J. 115
Mbiti, J. 48
McKenzie-Mavinga, I. 2, 4
methodology 73–77; autoethnography 1, 73, 75, 85; ethnographical approach 82–84; group discussions 89–93; questionnaire data collection 84–85, 87–89, 89; questionnaire participants 77–82, 85–87
missionaries *see* Christianity
Mogaji, A. 4, 106
Moodley, R. xi, 4, 107
Moustakas, C. 74, 85

Nigeria *see* country of 'Nigeria'

Obasi, M.E. 15
Obiechina, E. 40–45, 57–58, 64, 78, 134, 145
Object relations theorists 22, 70
oral tradition 14, 29–30, 43–46, 57–58, 62, 76–79, 123
Osaji, B. 68
Osuji, O. 105
Oyewole, A. 105, 115

Parron, D.L. *see* Hohmann, A. A.
Pedder, J. *see* Brown, D.
Pines, M. 62, 109, 130
Polanyi, M. 85
Prince, R.H. 116, 119, 122–123
psychotherapy: for Black and minority ethnic people xii, 62–63, 104–108, 128–133; and language xi, 59–63, 65–66, 113; and racism xi, 2, 4–5; *see also* group analysis

religion *see* African Traditional Religion (ATR); Christianity
rites, rituals and ceremonies 9–10, 24, 70, 78, 91–92; bird-shooting rite and

celebration (Igba Nnuna and Ignu Nnunu) 9–15, 73, 139; chieftaincy 10–12; marriage 12, 51–52, 98; *see also* healing
Rogers, C.R. 85

Scheff, T. 109–110, 132
Sedgewick, P. 108
Sodi, T. 119, 126–128, 129
Soyinka, W. 42, 44
Stacey, R. 21–22
Sue, D.W. 132
Sue, S. 130, 132
Swartz, L. 65–66, 110

Taiwo, C.O. 67
Torrey, E.P. 121
Turner, V.W. 127

Weber, M. 142
West African novelists 1, 8, 19, 42–45, 58, 146; *see also* Achebe, C.
Winnicott, D.W. 146

Yalom, I.D. 127
Yoruba nation and culture 2–3, 23, 36, 44, 68, 79; and language 68, 141–142; and modern psychiatry 111; and parenting 123

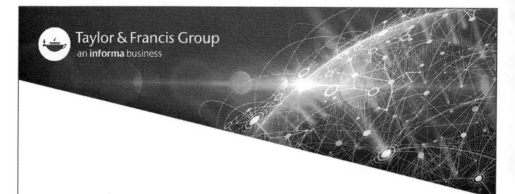